HeRbS

an A~Z guide

HeRbS

GARDENING,
COOKING &
HEALTH

Reader's
digest

The Reader's Digest Association, Inc.
New York, NY / Montreal

Contents

Introduction

Herbs have been used for thousands of years to flavour and preserve food, treat ailments, ward off pests and diseases, freshen the air, and decorate and enhance our lives. Over the centuries, they have also become associated with fascinating myths, legends and folklore.

In general terms, a herb is a plant that is valued for its flavour, aroma or medicinal properties, and different parts of a herb — such as the stalks, flowers, fruits, seeds, roots or leaves — may have important applications. From small herbs growing beside our highways and flowering garden favourites to creeping groundcovers, bushy shrubs, vines and tall trees, there are herbs to suit any location. Even if you live in an apartment with no outdoor space at all, you can still grow culinary herbs in a window box.

Herbs is a practical directory of more than 100 herbs, with their history, cultivation and their uses. It combines traditional knowledge, herbal wisdom and lore with up-to-date information on how to grow, harvest and store herbs and how to make the best of them in your daily life – in the kitchen, in beauty treatments, to improve your health and in your home by using fewer cleaning chemicals.

With easy-cooking recipes, gardening and harvesting tips, safe herbal remedies, natural beauty products, herbal cleaning items, craft ideas and intriguing snippets of herbal history, *Herbs* is packed with information and illustrated with beautiful photographs. We hope you will find it a source of inspiration.

The editors

Important

Growing herbs Some herbs can become invasive and may be toxic to livestock. This information has been given where possible, but regulations do change from time to time. Readers are advised to consult local plant services if they have any concerns.

Herbal medicine While the creators of this book have made every effort to be as accurate and up-to-date as possible, medical and pharmacological knowledge is constantly changing. Readers are advised to consult a qualified medical specialist for individual advice. Moreover, even though they are natural, herbs contain chemical substances that can sometimes have marked side effects. If used unwisely, they can be toxic. The writers, researchers, editors and publishers of this book cannot be held liable for any errors, omissions or actions that may be taken as a consequence of information contained in this book.

Enjoy the satisfaction of growing and harvesting your own herbs.

Aloe vera

The ancient Egyptians called aloe vera the 'plant of immortality'. The clear gel from the cut leaves has soothing, healing and hydrating properties, particularly for burns.

....

Latin names *Aloe vera* syn. *A. barbadensis,*
A. vulgaris Aloeaceae
Also known as Barbados aloe, bitter aloe,
Curacao aloe
Part used Leaves

Aloe vera

Gardening

Aloe vera is a succulent plant with fleshy light green leaves that create a fan from the stemless base. In warm climates, it produces narrow tubular yellow flowers.

• **Growing** Aloe requires a sunny position and a well-drained soil. Propagate it from the shoots that form at the base of the plant. Allow to dry for 2 days before planting them into small pots filled with a gritty, free-draining potting mix. Once they are well established, transfer them to their permanent position. Aloe is affected by even light frosts, and in areas where winter temperatures fall below 5°C, it is best grown as a pot plant and brought indoors in cool weather. It makes an excellent indoor plant in good light.

• **Harvesting and storing** Cut leaves when required, using only as much of the leaf as you need at the time.

Herbal medicine

Aloe vera. Part used: leaves. The clear gel squeezed from the centre of the aloe vera leaf is probably best known for its ability to encourage the speedy healing of burns. Native Americans called aloe vera 'the wand of heaven' and used it to treat sunburn. Not only does the cooling gel soothe the pain of burns, it also reduces inflammation. And if the skin is broken, aloe vera helps protect the burn site from infection as well as encouraging the skin's collagen to repair itself. The result is that burns heal more rapidly; in fact, researchers estimate that using aloe vera gel speeds up burn healing time by more than 8 days. Keep a plant on a sunny windowsill so that it's handy if you accidentally burn yourself while cooking. The gel can also be applied to minor wounds, abrasions, eczema, psoriasis and ulcers.

To use, apply fresh aloe vera gel to the affected area 3 times per day, or use a commercially prepared aloe vera skin cream, lotion or ointment. Avoid using small, young leaves, as the active constituents are most prevalent at about 3 years old. When shopping for commercial products, choose those certified by the International Aloe Science Council (IASC), which ensures the product is of high quality.

Do not take aloe vera internally. It can cause stomach cramping and diarrhoea and may interfere with the absorption of medications. Topical application is considered safe if you are pregnant or breastfeeding.

Natural beauty

Ultra-soothing and nourishing for even the most parched and dehydrated skin, aloe vera is also a mild exfoliant, gently removing dead skin cells and stimulating cell regeneration, helping to prevent scarring and diminish wrinkles.

Cleopatra used aloe vera juices to help preserve her beauty.

Softening anti-ageing hand mask

This softening and moisturising hand mask helps to even out skin tone and fade age spots.

1 tablespoon honey
3 tablespoons aloe vera gel
1 teaspoon lemon juice
10 drops lemon essential oil
almond meal, sufficient to make a paste

1 Melt honey over low heat. In a small bowl, combine the aloe vera gel with the honey and lemon juice. Add the essential oil and mix thoroughly.

2 Add sufficient almond meal to make a soft, workable paste; it should not be too sloppy. Smooth mask over clean hands, paying particular attention to the backs of hands and knuckles. Leave for 20 minutes. Rinse off with warm water and apply moisturiser.

Harvesting aloe vera gel

At their centre, aloe vera leaves contain a thick, colourless gel. This soothing gel is useful for treating burns and dry skin conditions. Use it fresh, as soon as you have harvested it, because it is unstable and quickly loses its consistency. Do not use any gel that has a green tinge.

1 Cut off a healthy large leaf close to its base.
2 Slice carefully along the centre of the leaf, along its entire length. Gently peel back the two cut edges. Use a blunt-edged knife to scrape the clear gel from the centre of the leaf, then place it in a bowl. You can also wrap the opened leaf around the problem area like a bandage.

Angelica

Angelica has both medicinal and culinary uses. Its name honours the archangel Raphael, who is said to have revealed to a monk that the plant could cure the plague.

Latin name *Angelica archangelica* Apiaceae
Also known as Archangel
Parts used Leaves, stems, seeds, roots

🍃 Gardening

A tall, showy and aromatic herb, *Angelica archangelica* is native to northern Europe and has been cultivated since ancient times for its medicinal properties. It grows to 1.2 m, has ribbed, hollow stems and bears flower clusters on long stems. Purple-stem angelica (*A. atropurpurea*) has similar uses to *A. archangelica*. It grows to about 1.8 m, has stems suffused with purple, and pale green to white flowers.

• **Growing** Angelica requires a shady position in well-drained but moist soil that has been enriched with compost. Allow a distance of 1 m between plants. Plants die once the seed has matured, but you can delay this by removing the emerging flower stem. First-year plants die back in winter but regrow in spring. Water regularly.

The flowers are attractive to many beneficial insects, including parasitoid wasps and lacewings.

• **Harvesting and storing** Harvest the leaves and flowering stalks in the second year. Dig the roots at the end of the second year, then wash and dry them. Gather the seed when brown and dry.

🍃 Herbal medicine

Angelica archangelica. Part used: roots. Angelica is an important digestive tonic in European herbal medicine. It stimulates the production of gastric juices and can relieve symptoms of poor appetite, dyspepsia and nausea. Angelica can also reduce the discomfort of flatulence, stomach cramps and bloating.

Angelica (*Angelica archangelica*)

For the safe and appropriate use of angelica, consult your healthcare professional. Do not use angelica in greater than culinary quantities.

🍃 Cooking

Boiled or steamed angelica leaf stalks are a popular vegetable dish in some Scandinavian countries; they have a musky, bittersweet taste. The dried seeds and stems are used (in maceration or via the essential oil) as a flavouring agent in vermouth and liqueurs such as Chartreuse and Benedictine. Crystallised leaves and young stems are a popular decoration for cakes and confectionery.

Blanch young shoots to use like celery in salads. Use leaves and stalks in marinades and in poaching liquids for seafood. Add leaves to recipes for tart fruits, such as rhubarb. They cut the acidity, and their sweetness allows you to reduce the amount of sugar. You can also add chopped leaves to fruit salads.

Anise

Anise provides much of the 'licorice' flavouring in bakery goods, teas, liqueurs, and chewing gum. Chinese star anise, although unrelated, has a similar flavour.

Latin name *Pimpinella anisum* Apiaceae
Also known as Aniseed, common anise
Parts used Roots (anise only), leaves, seeds, dried fruits (star anise only)

Anise (*Pimpinella anisum*)

🍃 Gardening

Anise is an aromatic annual with stalked, toothed leaves. The slender flowering stems bear clusters of small white flowers followed by ridged grey seeds.

Chinese star anise (*Illicium verum*), an evergreen tree, bears fruits that open to an 8-pointed star.

• **Growing** Anise prefers an enriched, light, well-drained soil. Sow anise seed directly in spring. Propagate Chinese star anise by semi-ripe cuttings; they will grow in well-drained but moist soil in light shade.

• **Harvesting and storing** Cut anise when the seeds are fully developed. Tie bunches inside paper bags and hang them upside-down to dry and catch the seed. Harvest star anise fruits just before ripening.

🍃 Cooking

Anise seeds and oil are used throughout Europe in drinks such as the French pastis, the Greek ouzo and Turkish raki. Use the seeds whole or crushed, but for the best flavour, grind them as you need them.

Use them in bakery goods, confectionery, tomato-based dishes, vegetable and seafood dishes, curries, pickles, soups, sauces and stews. Add the young leaves sparingly to green salads, fish dishes, fruit salads and cooked vegetables.

A culinary star

Star anise is an essential ingredient in many Asian cuisines. In Vietnamese cookery, it is used to flavour the noodle soup known as pho. Along with Sichuan pepper, cloves, cassia and fennel seeds, it is a component in Chinese five-spice mix (ingredients pictured right) and in Indian garam masala. You can use star anise whole, broken or ground. Add it to pork, chicken or duck stews. Insert a whole star anise into the cavity of a chicken or duck before roasting.

1. Sichuan pepper 2. Cassia 3. Cloves 4. Star anise
5. Fennel seeds

Anise hyssop

Many agastaches have fragrant foliage, their scents ranging from anise to mint and citrus. The leaves are used for herbal tea, flavouring and in medicines.

. . . .

Latin name *Agastache foeniculum* syn. *A. anethiodora* Lamiaceae
Also known as Anise mint, giant blue hyssop, licorice mint
Parts used Leaves, flowers

Gardening

Native to North America, anise hyssop (*A. foeniculum*) is a hardy perennial with a sweet anise scent. Both balsamic and peppermint–pennyroyal scented forms are available.

Korean mint (*A. rugosa*), similar to anise hyssop, is a short-lived perennial with a flower that ranges in colour from rose to violet.

Licorice mint (*A. rupestris*) is a perennial with small licorice-scented leaves and spikes of nectar-rich apricot flowers.

Hummingbird mint (*A. cana*) is a spectacular perennial growing to 90 cm with long, dense spikes of rosy pink flowers and aromatic foliage.

• **Growing** *A. foeniculum* and *A. rugosa* prefer light shade; most other species prefer a sunny position. Agastaches are easy to grow and are well-suited to pot culture. Sow seed in spring and cover lightly with soil. It usually takes 6 to 8 weeks to germinate. Pot on when large enough.

• **Harvesting and storing** Use the leaves and flowers freshly picked, or dry them by hanging them upside-down in small bunches away from direct sunlight. They will retain their colour and scent.

Agastache is from the Greek word for 'very much' and 'ear of wheat'.

Cooking

The flowers of anise hyssop yield large quantities of nectar, which was popular with North American beekeepers in the 19th century for producing a faintly aniseed-flavoured honey. Native Americans used it as a tea and a sweetener.

Infuse the dried leaves to make a hot or cold drink. Also, use them to season lamb, chicken or salmon. Add the seeds to cakes and muffins. Use the flowers or fresh leaves of anise hyssop or Korean mint in fruit and leaf salads. Korean mint has a peppermint and aniseed flavour and aroma and is a good substitute for mint.

Anise hyssop (*Agastache foeniculum* syn. *A. anethiodora*)

Arnica

There are about 30 species of *Arnica*, all of them are perennials. With its cheerful, daisy-like flowers, arnica has long been used to treat bruises and sprains.

Latin name *Arnica montana* Asteraceae
Also known as Leopard's bane, mountain tobacco
Part used Flowers

Gardening

From late spring to late summer, *Arnica montana* produces flowering stems up to 60 cm high, each bearing a single, golden flower. Native to subalpine woods and pastures of Europe, the plant is becoming rare in the wild, due to over-collection and the inroads of agriculture, and wild collection is being curtailed. As a result, the American species *A. chamissonis* is often used in its place in herbal treatment.

• **Growing** Arnica requires a cool climate, full sun and free-draining soil. Arnica is a slow grower. Mulch well and weed regularly, or grow plants in weed mat.

• **Harvesting and storing** Gather the flowers when fully open and dry them.

Arnica (*Arnica montana*)

Herbal medicine

Arnica montana, A. chamissonis. Part used: flowers. Arnica flowers have significant anti-inflammatory and mild analgesic properties and the plant has a long history of use as a topical treatment to stimulate the healing of muscles and other soft tissues after trauma.

Arnica is available in the form of infused oil and commercially available ointments and creams which are applied to bruises, sprains and strains to encourage healing and help reduce the discomfort of pain and swelling. The pain-relieving effects of arnica also make it a suitable topical remedy for the treatment of sore and aching muscles and rheumatic joint problems.

Choose a product that contains 10 to 20 per cent arnica tincture or oil. As long as the skin is not broken, apply the cream, ointment or infused oil to the affected area 3 times per day, using small circular motions to massage it in.

Do not use arnica in any form if you are pregnant or breastfeeding.

Soothe sports injuries

Strains and sprains occur when excessive force causes muscles and tendons to stretch beyond their normal range, resulting in pain and inflammation. Some athletes report that arnica helps reduce the pain and speeds up the healing of sports injuries. They also note that their bruises change colour more quickly.

Artemisia

Artemisia is a genus containing about 300 species, although few are grown in gardens. A number of species inhibit other plants, sometimes to the point of death.

....

Latin name *Artemisia* sp. Asteraceae
Also known as *Artemisia absinthium*: wormwood, old woman. *A. pontica*: Roman wormwood, old warrior. *A. abrotanum*: southernwood, lad's love, maiden's ruin, old man. *A. afra*: wilde als
Parts used Aerial parts, roots

Gardening

Wormwood (*A. absinthium*) forms a woody shrub to about 80 cm with a bittersweet smell. Its deeply incised grey-green leaves are covered in fine hairs.

Tree wormwood (*A. arborescens*) resembles wormwood but grows upright to about 1.5 to 1.8 m, with narrower leaf segments; it smells less strongly.

Roman wormwood (*A. pontica*) is a low-growing plant to about 40 cm, with finely cut, scented leaves.

White sage or native wormwood (*A. ludoviciana*) has silvered foliage. and is an aromatic upright subshrub to 1.2 m that is used as an ornamental.

Mugwort (*A. vulgaris*) is a perennial that grows to about 90 cm, with deeply incised leaves that are deep green above and greyish white below.

Wilde als (*A. afra*) is indigenous to Africa, from the Western Cape up to Ethiopia. A popular garden plant, it forms clumpy bushes from 0.5 to 2 m.

• **Growing** Most species prefer full sun and good drainage, although mugwort tolerates partial shade. As it is strongly insecticidal, use artemisia as a companion plant in the edge of gardens.

• **Harvesting and storing** Harvest the leaves as required to use fresh or dried.

Herbal medicine

A. absinthium. Parts used: aerial parts. Wormwood is used to treat symptoms associated with poor digestion. In some cultures it is regarded as a remedy for worm infestations and other parasitic infections of the gut.

For the safe and appropriate use of artemisia, consult your healthcare professional. Do not use these herbs if you are pregnant or breastfeeding.

Tree wormwood
(*Artemisia arborescens*)

Design for a formal herb garden

- This formal herb garden has a classic symmetrical layout, with the height elements provided by an olive tree in each corner and trellises on either side.
- The main colour scheme is lavender and mauve flowers, with grey-green foliage provided by lavender, artemisia, olive and rosemary.

- The central herb garden is planted with culinary herbs, but you could also use the four quadrants to separate culinary from medicinal herbs, for instance.
- The standard roses on either side of the entrance are reminders of how, in their monastic gardens, monks grew standard roses to represent themselves at work.

Basil

While sweet basil, with its savoury clove fragrance, is the quintessential Italian herb, basils are available in an amazing range of fragrances from lemon to sweet camphor.

....

Latin name *Ocimum* sp. Lamiaceae
Parts used Leaves, flower spikes

Sweet basil (*Ocimum basilicum*)

🍃 Gardening

There are 64 basil species, all native to the subtropics and tropics. They have aromatic leaves and spikes of lipped flowers arranged in whorls. Most are annuals, but there are also evergreen perennials and shrubs. Best-known is sweet basil (*O. basilicum*), and many varieties have been developed, particularly in the Mediterranean region.

Compact small-leafed forms of *O. basilicum* are popular in Greece and for pot and windowsill culture.

Large-leafed sweet basils include 'Lettuce Leaf' and 'Mammoth'. Both have leaves that are large enough to use as food wraps.

Coloured-leaf forms are widely used as ornamental plantings as well as for culinary purposes.

Citrus-flavoured varieties include lemon basil (*O. americanum*). Hybrid varieties (*O.* x *citriodorum*) include 'Sweet Dani' and 'Mrs Burn's Lemon', which are richly lemon-scented and ideal for culinary use.

Strongly spice-scented varieties of *O. basilicum* include 'Oriental Breeze', a purple-flowered form much used for ornamental and culinary purposes; and 'Spice' (often incorrectly sold as 'Holy Basil'), with its heady, almost incense-like fragrance. 'Sacred Basil' or 'Holy Basil' (*O. tenuiflorum* syn. *O. sanctum*), which is available in both green- and purple-leafed strains, has a mild spice scent and is widely planted in India around temples and in gardens. 'Anise Basil' (*O. basilicum*), also sold as 'Licorice Basil', has a sweet anise scent and purple-suffused leaves. The basil encountered in the cooking of Thailand and Vietnam, 'Thai Basil' (*O. basilicum*), has a light, sweet anise scent, glossy green foliage and ornamental lavender flowers.

Some handsome perennial basils are the result of hybridisation between *O. basilicum* and *O. kilimandscharicum*, the camphor-scented perennial

'Dark Opal', a variety of *O. basilicum*, bears long cerise flowers and has a delicate scent.

Making pesto

Pesto is a showcase for fresh basil. Pistou, the French variation of this Italian sauce, is made without pine nuts.

Use 2 fat cloves garlic, peeled, 30 g pine nuts, ¼ cup (25 g) freshly grated parmesan or pecorino cheese, 4 heaped tablespoons fresh basil leaves (tough stalks removed) and 3 tablespoons good-quality olive oil.

Process dry ingredients roughly. Add oil in a steady stream; mixture should be slightly grainy. Add more oil, if needed. Pack in a jar; top with a film of olive oil. Seal; refrigerate. Use within 2 weeks.

species. They have a spicy clove fragrance and include the white-flowered, green-leafed 'All Year' basil, and the beautiful purple-suffused 'African Blue'.

Tree basil or East Indian basil (*O. gratissimum*) is pleasantly thyme- and clove-scented and makes a substantial bush to about 1.5 m. Another strain of this species, sold as 'Mosquito Plant' or 'Fever Plant', has a strong thyme scent.

• Growing Basils require a protected, warm, sunny site with a well-drained soil. Water regularly. Being a tropical plant, basil grows rapidly at temperatures in excess of 16°C and is frost-sensitive. Pinch out flower heads to promote bushy plant growth and to prolong the plant's productive life.

Consider planting basils among other plants, rather than en masse. They make a fashionable addition to the ornamental garden.

• Harvesting and storing Harvest mature leaves and flower spikes for fresh use at any time. To dry the leaves, cut bushes at the base and hang out of direct light, then store in an airtight container in a cool place.

Around the home

Basil is a natural disinfectant. Use the essential oil in combination with other antiseptic herbal oils to make disinfectant sprays for cleaning household surfaces. Plant basil in a pot close to the back door to deter flies. Cut a bunch of basil as an aromatic table centrepiece when you eat outdoors. The dried flower heads add a sweet and spicy note to a pot-pourri.

Cooking

Basil is one of the great culinary herbs; different varieties are used extensively in both European and Asian cooking. If a recipe specifies simply 'basil', sweet or common basil (*Ocimum basilicum*) is the type generally meant. Fresh sweet basil is highly aromatic, with a distinctive scent and flavour reminiscent of aniseed, and tends to be either loved or loathed. Dried basil tastes more of curry, and is a poor substitute for the fresh herb and should be avoided.

In Greece, pots of Greek basil (*Ocimum minimum* 'Greek') are placed on outside tables to deter flies.

Classically Italian

Insalata Caprese ('salad in the style of Capri'), in the colours of the Italian flag, is a light, summery salad that showcases the flavour of basil and ripe tomatoes. Arrange tomato slices on a plate. Intersperse with slices of fresh bocconcini (baby mozzarella). Season well. Add a dash of olive oil and a scattering of fresh basil leaves.

Using a knife to cut basil can bruise and darken the leaves. For salads and pasta sauces where appearance matters, shred the leaves with your fingers. Young leaves have the best flavour, while old ones have a coarser, stronger taste.

In cooked dishes, basil quickly loses its aroma and the leaves tend to darken, so add it to give depth of flavour during cooking and then, for fragrance and visual appeal, stir in a little more just before serving. Tomato dishes, chicken, egg and rice dishes, spaghetti sauces, fish and vegetables — especially beans, capsicum and eggplants — all go well with basil.

Basil is a good addition to stuffings. The most famous use of basil is in pesto (or pistou in French). Citrus-scented and spice-flavoured varieties of basil work well in a range of Asian recipes.

Aromatic basil oil

Preserve basil the Italian way. Layer the leaves in a jar and sprinkle each layer with salt. Then top up the jar with good-quality olive oil. Seal the jar securely and store in the refrigerator, allowing several days for the oil to be infused with the flavour of the basil. Use the leaves and the oil for making pesto (see recipe, *page 19*). Drizzle a little oil over pizzas or salads. Also, try adding a dash to a marinade.

> *'A man taking basil from a woman will love her always.'*
>
> Sir Thomas More
> Tudor statesman and philosopher, 1478–1535

A herb of contradictions

Basil has both positive and negative associations that include love and fear, danger and protection, and life and death. The negative connotations may come from basil's Latin epithet *basilicum*, which links the plant to the basilisk, the mythical serpent with the deadly gaze. The ancient Greeks and Romans believed it necessary to swear loudly and utter curses when sowing basil to ensure its successful germination.

Its heart-shaped leaves have made basil a symbol of love.

Bay

The bay is a long-lived and slow-growing, pyramid-shaped evergreen tree. According to folklore, a bay tree in the garden keeps away evil as well as thunder and lightning.

Latin name *Laurus nobilis* Lauraceae
Also known as Bay laurel, Grecian bay, sweet bay
Parts used Leaves, flower buds, fruits, bark, roots

Gardening

While a bay tree can reach about 15 m over a long period, its slow, dense upright growth habit makes it an ideal specimen for a large pot, whether it is allowed to grow into its natural form or shaped into an ornamental topiary or standard. In this form, a small garden can accommodate a bay without concern; its growth is even slower when cultivated in a pot. A single tree, even when kept small by pruning, should provide more than enough leaves for a household. Bay generally flowers only in warm climates, and the small, very fragrant flower buds open to tiny cream flowers.

• **Growing** Bay trees prefer a deep soil, so if you are growing one in a pot, plant it in one of generous depth, in a compost-enriched potting mix. Provide full sun and good air circulation. Bay trees prefer a rich, well-drained but moist position. Plants grown without adequate ventilation and light can develop disfiguring grey mildew, which should be treated with sulfur while the plant is wet with morning dew.

• **Harvesting and storing** Pick green leaves for use at any time. Leaves that you plan to dry should be collected on a dry, sunny morning before flowering has started. Choose a time after the dew has evaporated, but before the sun gets too hot and starts causing the essential oils in the plant to evaporate. Remove any dirt by gently brushing the leaves, but don't wash them in water. Discard any leaves that look diseased or damaged.

Bay (*Laurus nobilis*)

Beef and potato hotpot

1 kg piece of braising beef, such as chuck

100 g bacon, diced

3–4 small onions, cut into wedges

4 sprigs fresh thyme, leaves picked

2 fresh bay leaves

1 cup (250 ml) dry red wine

½ cup (125 ml) salt-reduced beef stock

750 g small boiling (waxy) or all-purpose potatoes, peeled and sliced

4 carrots, sliced

1 Remove sinews and fat from the beef. Pat dry with paper towel and rub on all sides with salt and black pepper.

2 Fry bacon in large flameproof casserole dish or heavy-based saucepan over high heat without oil. Add beef and brown on all sides. Add onions and fry until well browned, stirring constantly. Sprinkle thyme over the beef and place bay leaves on top.

3 Pour in wine and stir to loosen the solids from the bottom of the dish. Add the stock and bring to the boil. Reduce heat to low; cover and simmer for 1½ hours, turning beef occasionally. Season with salt and black pepper.

4 Add potatoes and carrots. Cover and simmer for 30 minutes, or until vegetables are tender.

5 Remove beef, carve into slices and place back in the dish with the vegetables. Season to taste and serve hot from the dish.

SERVES 4 to 6

Bouquet garni, a bundle of classic herbs, usually includes bay, thyme, parsley and peppercorns.

If you've collected sprigs of leaves, strip the lower leaves from each stem, tie the stems together and hang the bunches upside-down.

Keep the leaves in a warm, airy place away from sunlight, and check them everyday or so until they have completely dried.

Cooking

Sweet bay is indispensable in French and other Mediterranean cookery. The tough leaves withstand long cooking, so use them in soups and stews. Apart from meat and fish, they go well in dishes that contain lentils or beans. Two leaves are sufficient in a dish that serves six people.

Bay is essential in a bouquet garni, which is made with fresh herbs or dried herbs wrapped in muslin. Bay is also used in pickling spice and garam masala.

Fresh leaves tend to be bitter, but the taste will diminish if they are left to wilt for a few days. Fresh sprigs stripped of a few leaves make aromatic skewers for meat or fish cooked on the barbecue.

Dried leaves retain their flavour for about a year. Remove dried leaves from dishes before serving.

History and myth

The bay tree was considered sacred to the sun god Apollo, and later to his son Asclepius, the Greek god of medicine. According to myth, Apollo fell in love with Daphne, a beautiful nymph who, rather than returning his affection, appealed to the gods to rescue her from him. She was duly changed into a bay tree, the perfect disguise. Apollo declared the tree sacred and thereafter wore a bay laurel wreath in Daphne's honour.

Bay has long been considered a herb of strong magic, able to attract good fortune and wealth, and to keep away evil. The death of bay trees was considered a portent of evil times; when the city of Rome fell to invasion from the north in the 4th century, all the bay trees are reputed to have died.

During outbreaks of the plague Roman citizens burned bay leaves in the public squares, and the herb was used for this purpose into the 16th century.

The leaves are mildly narcotic in quantity; it is said that the Oracle of Delphi in Greece chewed bay leaves before she entered a prophetic trance.

Around the home

To deter weevils in your pantry, add a few bay leaves to containers of flour and rice. Bay leaves placed between the pages of a book may also help to repel silverfish. As the leaves will lose their pungency, they need to be regularly replaced.

A cake rake covered with kitchen paper is ideal for drying individual leaves, or you could stretch mesh over a frame.

Bergamot

Native Americans used the fragrant leaves of *Monarda* to make medicinal tisanes to treat mouth and throat infections and to ease the discomfort of colic and flatulence.

Latin name *Monarda* sp. Laminaceae
Also known as Bee balm, Monarda, Oswego tea
Part used Leaves

Wild bergamot (*Monarda fistulosa*)

🍃 Gardening

Monarda, a member of the mint family, is native to North America and obtained its common name because the scent of its foliage resembled that of the bergamot orange (*Citrus bergamia* syn. *C. aurantium* var. *bergamia*), a small citrus tree grown mainly in Italy.

The leaf fragrances of *Monarda* range from oregano to lemon. Oswego tea (*M. didyma*), a perennial, grows to 1.2 m, and bears dense whorls of long-tubed, scarlet flowers; the leaves have a very pleasant citrus scent. Wild bergamot (*M. fistulosa*) has lance-shaped leaves and whorled heads of lavender (and occasionally pink) flowers; different strains have thyme- or rose geranium-scented leaves. Most garden bergamots are hybrids and include varieties such as 'Blue Stocking' and 'Mohawk'.

- **Growing** Bergamots prefer a sunny position and an enriched, moist but well-drained soil. Propagate by seed, or by dividing perennials in early spring. You can also take stem cuttings in summer.
- **Harvesting and storing** Harvest the edible flowers as required. Collect leaves in late spring and dry them.

🍃 Herbal medicine

Monarda didyma, *M. fistulosa*. Part used: leaves.
M. didyma has long been used by Native Americans as a general stimulant. After the Boston Tea Party, in 1773, when American colonists dumped tea shipped by the British East India Company in protest against British rule, the bergamot tea of the Oswego Indians became a popular substitute. Bergamot is reputed to contain thymol, an essential oil compound also found in thyme and marjoram, which has a calming effect on the digestive system, and the plant has been used medicinally to ease flatulence and colic.

For the safe and appropriate use of bergamot, consult your healthcare professional. Do not use these herbs if you are pregnant or breastfeeding.

Oswago tea bergamot (*Monarda didyma*)

Bergamot orange

The intensely fragrant waxy white flowers of the European bergamot orange, borne in clusters in spring, are the source of the essential oil of neroli, used widely in the perfumery trade and an ingredient in eau de cologne, a mixture of citrus oils that dates from the early 18th century. Bergamot orange's bitter but highly aromatic yellow peel is used to flavour Earl Grey tea.

The nectar-rich blossoms of Oswego tea bergamot attract bees and honey-seeking birds.

Borage

Considered a cure for 'melancholia' in ancient times, borage is an excellent companion plant, helping to deter pests and stimulating the growth of strawberries.

Latin name *Borago officinalis* Boraginaceae
Also known as Starflower
Parts used Leaves, flowers

The age of chivalry

During the Crusades, borage was infused in stirrup cups and offered to Crusaders about to depart for the Holy Land, in the belief that it would grant them courage. Ladies traditionally embroidered its star-like flowers onto scarves, which they gave to their chosen knights before they went into combat.

Gardening

Borage, a large-leaved annual, bears five-petalled, intense blue flowers on stems up to 90 cm. The whole plant has a cucumber scent, is coarsely hairy and can irritate sensitive skin.

• **Growing** Borage requires a sunny, well-drained position and prefers a well-dug and composted soil. Sow plants directly into the ground in spring and in autumn. You can sow them in pots, but you should transplant them while they are young, as they develop a large taproot.

• **Harvesting and storing** Harvest borage year round as required. Dry the leaves in a very cool oven or in a well-aired place, out of direct sunlight.

Herbal medicine

Borago officinalis. Part used: seed oil. Borage seed oil is a source of gamma-linolenic acid (GLA), an omega-6 fatty acid also found in evening primrose oil which may be of therapeutic value in the treatment of dry and itching skin conditions, including eczema and psoriasis. The latest evidence suggests that better therapeutic results may be achieved when GLA and other omega-6 oils are taken in combination with omega-3 essential fatty acids, such as those found in flax seed and fish.

The leaves are used as a poultice for sprains, bruises and inflammation, and in facial steams for dry skin.

Do not use borage seed oil if you are pregnant or breastfeeding.

Cooking

Remove the sepals from flowers and use them in salads, or crystallise for use as cake decorations.

Borage (*Borago officinalis*)

Brahmi

This tropical herb is reputed to improve both brain function and memory. Brahmi makes an attractive hanging basket. You can also grow it in an ornamental pond.

Latin name *Bacopa monnieri* Scrophulaceae
Also known as Bacopa, thyme-leafed gratiola, water hyssop
Parts used Whole plant above ground

🌿 Gardening

Bright green brahmi is a modest ground-hugging perennial plant that grows in wetland environments. It is slightly succulent and bears small five-petalled flowers that are white, faintly tinged blue on the petal backs, over many months.

● **Growing** Brahmi grows well in a pot, preferably with a diameter of 30 cm or more, and makes an attractive hanging basket if grown in the shade. Brahmi forms adventitious roots on creeping shoots, and the detached shoots quickly grow into new plants when potted. Water regularly, especially if exposed to direct hot sunshine.

● **Harvesting and storing** Harvest stems and leaves when the plant is 5 months old, leaving 5-cm stems to allow the plant to regenerate for further harvesting. Dry leaves in the shade at room temperature and store in airtight containers.

🌿 Herbal medicine

Bacopa monnieri. Parts used: whole herb. Brahmi is said to improve memory, learning and concentration. Scientific research has provided encouraging evidence for some of these effects, but suggests improvements take around 3 months to occur. Brahmi is

Food for the brain

Keeping our brains healthy is as important as keeping our bodies in shape. Brahmi has been used as a 'brain workout' herb in Eastern herbal medicine for about 500 years. Researchers hypothesise that it may help by improving the way the nervous system transmits messages in the brain.

Gotu kola (*Centella asiatica* syn. *Hydrocotyle asiatica*) is also sometimes confusingly referred to by the common name brahmi and is a 'brain' herb in its own right. However, the two plants are easily distinguished by their different leaf shapes (see Gotu kola, *page 87*).

also renowned as an exceptional nerve tonic, so it is notable that a reduction in anxiety levels was also observed in some clinical studies, supporting its use during times of anxiety and nervous exhaustion.

Do not use brahmi if you are pregnant or you are breastfeeding.

Brahmi (*Bacopa monnieri*)

Burdock

Although regarded as a weed in the northern hemisphere, burdock is enjoying a resurgence in popularity, both as a vegetable and a traditional medicinal plant.

....

Latin name *Arctium lappa* Asteraceae
Also known as Beggar's buttons, great burdock
Parts used Leaves, roots, seeds

Burdock (*Arctium lappa*)

🍃 Gardening

Burdock is a strong-growing biennial. The fairly bitter but tender young foliage of spring regrowth is used as a green vegetable. The leaves are large and oval, and the numerous purple thistle-like flowers are quite remarkable in their perfect symmetry. Burdock can grow as high as 2.4 m and thrives in full sun. Propagate from seed in spring or late autumn.

• **Harvesting and storing** For cooking, collect young shoots and leaves in spring. Lift the roots in autumn, about 100 days after planting, when they are at least 30 cm long. For medicinal purposes, dry the greyish brown roots, which are white on the inside.

🍃 Herbal medicine

Arctium lappa. Part used: roots. In Western herbal medicine, burdock root is used as an alterative or blood purifier. These terms describe its gentle detoxifying effect on the body and stimulation of the body's lymphatic, digestive and urinary systems. Herbalists also prescribe burdock root for chronic inflammatory skin and joint conditions, and when used over a long period of time it can help to clear dry, scaly skin complaints, such as eczema and psoriasis, and improve rheumatic joint conditions.

For the safe and appropriate use of burdock, consult your healthcare professional. Do not use burdock if you are pregnant or breastfeeding.

🍃 Cooking

Burdock is not an important edible plant. The cultivated Japanese form, known as gobo, is grown for its slender, crisp, textured taproot, which can grow as long as 1.3 m. It has a flavour between that of parsnip and Jerusalem artichoke and is eaten as a vegetable and also used in various pickles and a miso-based condiment. The taproot is also eaten as a vegetable in Korea.

Scrape the young leaf stalks and cook them as you would celery. Use the roots raw as a salad vegetable, or cooked in stir-fries like carrots.

Making it stick

The evenly distributed hooks on the burdock burrs, which kept sticking to his clothes on walks in the countryside, inspired George de Mestral to invent Velcro in 1945. The name comes from the French words *velour*, meaning 'velvet' and *crochet* or 'hook'. The invention has been applied to a wide range of items, from fasteners on clothes, bags and shoes to stainless steel hook and loop fasteners that are used to attach car parts.

Calendula

In ancient Rome, calendula was used to make a broth that was said to uplift the spirits. In India, the bright flowers decorated the altars in Hindu temples.

Calendula (*Calendula officinalis*)

Latin name *Calendula officinalis* Asteraceae
Also known as Golds, marigold, pot marigold, ruddles
Part used Petals

Gardening

Native to the Mediterranean, calendula forms a clump of aromatic leaves. The large, daisy-like flowers are golden yellow or orange. The original calendula of the herb garden was the single form; however, in the 20th century, double-flowered forms were extensively bred, yielding much larger harvests of medicinally valuable petals. An heirloom single variety from the Elizabethan period that is still grown is the quaint 'Hen and Chickens' *C. officinalis* 'Prolifera', which has a central flower encircled by a number of smaller flowers.

• **Growing** Calendula is an annual that is very easy to grow from seed. Plants need full sun but will tolerate partial light shade. They prefer a well-drained soil. Regular deadheading will help to prolong flowering.

• **Harvesting and storing** Gather petals after the dew has dried and spread them very thinly over paper on racks, out of direct sunlight, in a well-ventilated place. When they are dried, store in airtight containers.

Herbal medicine

Calendula officinalis. Part used: flowers. Brightly coloured calendula flowers possess significant wound-healing and local anti-inflammatory properties. To aid the healing of wounds, cuts and burns, apply them topically in the form of an ointment, cream or infused oil (see following page). Calendula's slight astringency may help to staunch bleeding, while its antimicrobial effects help to keep the site of injury free from infection. Use a calendula tincture as an effective mouthwash against gum infections and mouth ulcers.

Traditionally, calendula flowers are taken internally for infections and inflammation of the gut. For internal use, consult your healthcare professional.

Do not take calendula internally if you are pregnant or breastfeeding. Topical application is considered safe.

Globetrotting

Pot marigold should not be confused with the Mexican genus (*Tagetes*), which includes the so-called African and French marigolds (above) as well as the coriander-tasting Andean herb huacatay or Peruvian black mint (*Tagetes terniflora*), and the closely related *T. minuta*.

Calendula-infused oil

This cold infusion process is ideal for extracting oil-soluble components from fragile or delicate plant parts, such as flowers, petals and leaves.

1　Pack a wide-necked, clear glass jar with fresh or dried herb (fresh calendula flowers are used here), leaving about 1 cm space at the top of the jar. Pour vegetable oil (such as olive oil) over the herb until it is covered to a depth of about 5 mm. Stir gently.

2　Fold some fine muslin and place on top of the oil. Seal the lid tightly and give the bottle a good shake. Store in a warm, sunny place for 3 to 10 days. Shake the bottle several times a day.

3　Filter the oil through fine muslin into a clean jug. Squeeze as much oil as possible through the remaining pulp. If any sediment remains in the oil, cover the jug and leave the oil to stand for a day or two until the sediment settles to the bottom.

4　Gently pour the oil into a dark glass bottle, taking care to leave the sediment layer behind. Seal; label with the name of the herb and the date.

Usage Apply the infused oil topically as is or add it to a cream or ointment.

Storage Store in a cool, dark place for up to 6 months, but discard at the first sign of rancidity or fermentation.

Caraway

Caraway was a popular Middle Eastern herb before being introduced into Western Europe in the 12th century. It is used in cooking and medicinally to relieve bloating.

Latin name *Carum carvi* Apiaceae
Also known as Persian cumin
Parts used Leaves, roots, dried ripe fruits (known as seeds) and their essential oil

Gardening

Caraway is a biennial with fern-like leaves and a parsley–dill fragrance. It has a spindle-shaped taproot, which can be cooked as a root vegetable, like carrot. The flowering stem, about 60 cm tall, bears tiny white flowers touched with pink that are followed by crescent-shaped ridged 'seeds'.
C. roxburghianum, known as ajmud, is a popular Indian spice. 'Sprinter' is high-yielding, and the seeds don't shatter when dry, making it easier to save the seeds.

- **Growing** Caraway requires a well-drained fertile soil and a warm sunny position. Sow caraway seed directly into the soil in either spring or autumn (the latter crop will seed the following summer). Regularly weed and water the crop, as the seed is often slow to germinate. Thin plants to 15 cm apart. Caraway is rarely troubled by pests.
- **Harvesting and storing** As it is a biennial, caraway takes two seasons to produce seed. Lift roots after harvesting seed. Cut flowering stems when the seeds begin to darken and ripen. Secure stems in small bunches to allow air movement, and hang the bunches upside-down until dry. Then shake bunches over sheets. The seeds often contain insects, such as weevils, so freeze them to kill the eggs before storage. You can gather leaves at any time.

Caraway (*Carum carvi*)

Herbal medicine

Carum carvi. Part used: dried ripe fruits. Caraway's ability to dispel wind and, like peppermint (see *page 125*), exert a calming, antispasmodic effect on the gastrointestinal tract makes it a reliable remedy in cases of flatulence, intestinal colic and bloating. The essential oils of the two herbs are sometimes combined in commercial products.

Additionally, because of its slightly drying nature, it is often prescribed with other appropriate herbs to assist in the relief of diarrhoea.

Cooking

The entire caraway plant is edible. The anise-scented seeds are used to flavour rye bread, sausages, cabbage dishes, cheeses, soups, pork dishes, goulash and cooked apples, as well as liqueurs and spirits such as schnapps. A digestive known as 'sugar plums' is made from sugar-coated seeds.

Use the feathery caraway leaves in salads and soups. Their taste resembles a mixture of parsley and dill. The roots can be cooked and eaten like carrots.

Caraway crackers

Preheat oven to 200°C. Roll out 400 g ready-made pizza dough or puff pastry to 5 mm thickness on a lightly floured work surface. Whisk 1 egg yolk with 2 tablespoons water until combined and brush lightly over dough. Cut dough into 5 cm squares. Combine 2 tablespoons each of poppy seeds, caraway seeds, sunflower seeds and chopped almonds. Sprinkle over squares. Bake for 10 to 15 minutes, or until pastry is golden. Serve warm.

MAKES 36

Caraway seeds add a distinctive flavour to rye bread.

Bavarian cabbage salad

1 kg tender green cabbage

1 teaspoon salt

1 tablespoon caraway seeds

100 g piece of speck or bacon, rind removed, finely diced

3 tablespoons vegetable oil

3–4 tablespoons white wine vinegar

freshly ground black pepper

1 teaspoon sugar

3 tablespoons snipped fresh chives, and a few whole chives to garnish

1   Remove core from cabbage. Shred leaves finely with a knife or grate with a cheese grater.

2   Place 2 litres water in a large saucepan with salt and the caraway seeds. Bring to the boil. Add the shredded cabbage; cook for 2 minutes. Drain cabbage in a colander; refresh under cold running water. Leave to drain and cool completely.

3   Heat 1 tablespoon oil in a heavy-based pan over high heat. Add speck and cook on all sides until crisp. Combine speck with cabbage in a serving bowl.

4   Whisk remaining 2 tablespoons oil, vinegar, a little salt, black pepper and the sugar in a bowl until well combined. Stir vinaigrette into salad. Cover and chill for 45 minutes to allow flavours to develop.

5   Just before serving, taste salad and adjust seasonings. Serve garnished with chopped and whole chives.

SERVES 4

Catnip

Many cats that encounter this velvety, curiously scented plant react by rolling in it, rubbing against it and generally behaving as though the aroma is irresistible.

....

Latin name *Nepeta cataria* Lamiaceae
Part used Leaves

🍃 Gardening

Catnip is a short-lived perennial native to Europe that resembles its relative, mint. It has soft, hairy, aromatic grey-green leaves and small, white, lipped flowers. The chemicals responsible for the amazing response of many cats are nepetalactones. A lemon-scented variety, *N. cataria* var. *citriodora*, has a similar effect. Not all cats exhibit such reactions: young kittens and older cats show almost no response.

- **Growing** Catnip needs a well-drained soil, and preferably full sun. Grow from seed, if possible in seed trays, and after transplanting the seedlings, cover them with wire netting to protect them from the attentions of felines. Plants grow rapidly in summer to form quite large, floppy bushes, so you'll need to stake them. Water regularly.

- **Harvesting and storing** Once the bush is well-grown, you can harvest catnip at any time after the dew has dried. Secure small bunches of stems with string and hang them upside-down in a well-aired place. When perfectly dry, strip the foliage and store it in an airtight container.

🍃 Herbal medicine

Nepeta cataria. Parts used: leaves, flowers. An excellent remedy for children, catnip helps to resolve feverish conditions, and its antispasmodic properties alleviate flatulence and colic. It is a mild sedative and can reduce sensitivity to the pain of teething.

Catnip can also be used to treat the symptoms of colds, flu, digestive bloating, nausea and cramping in adults, and it is particularly effective when stress is a contributing factor.

For the safe and appropriate use of catnip, consult a healthcare professional. Do not use catnip if you are pregnant or breastfeeding.

🍃 Around the home

Catnip is a useful herb to have on hand in the home. Nepetalactones are a very powerful mosquito repellent and cockroaches don't like them much, either.

Catnip cat toy

Trace a fish outline onto some thin cardboard and cut out a template. Place two fabric rectangles right sides together. Trace the fish onto the wrong side of one rectangle, remembering to add 6-mm seam allowance all round.

Stitch the two shapes together, leaving a small opening for turning. Trim seam, clip curves and turn right side out. Fill with dried catnip and stitch opening closed. Stitch a small bell to the head of the fish.

Celery

Rich in vitamins, wild celery has been valued as a food since ancient Egyptian times. The Greeks crowned victors in the Nemean Games with garlands of its leaves.

Latin name *Apium graveolens* Apiaceae
Also known as Cutting leaf celery, smallage
Parts used Leaves, seeds, roots

Gardening

The deep green leaves of wild celery may reach 80 cm, while the flowering stems bear clusters of small, white-tinged green flowers. The whole plant, including the tiny brown seeds, is very aromatic. Chinese celery or kin tsai (*A. graveolens*), although sharing the same scientific name, is more strongly flavoured, with thin stalks that can be dark green to white in colour. *A. prostratum* is a creeping, shiny-leaved, somewhat succulent Australian coastal plant with a strong celery flavour. It is used as a flavouring in commercial bush foods.

• **Growing** Celery prefers a well-drained soil enriched with rotted compost and a sunny but protected position, and is tolerant of saline soils. Grow from seed in spring. Space plants to about 40 cm apart. Keep the soil moist with regular watering.

• **Harvesting and storing** Harvest leaves from midsummer to autumn, as required. Pick ripe seeds, then dry, deep-freeze for several days to kill any insect eggs, and store in an airtight container.

Herbal medicine

Apium graveolens. Part used: dried ripe fruits (seeds). Celery seed has a strong diuretic effect and enhances elimination of uric acid and other toxins from the body via the urinary system. This action may help to explain its use as a specific remedy for the treatment of painful joint conditions, such as gout and arthritis, in which an accumulation of toxins in the joint area may be partly responsible for the characteristic symptoms of pain and swelling. For the treatment of gout, boil 0.5 to 2 g of dried celery seed in a cup of water for 10 minutes to make a decoction; drink up to 3 times daily. Commercial preparations are also available.

As a result of its diuretic properties, celery seed can be used to treat fluid retention. Due to its slightly antiseptic nature, it can be of assistance in treating urinary tract infections.

Do not use celery seed in greater than culinary quantities if you are pregnant or breastfeeding.

Cooking

Celery's tiny edible seeds are aromatic and slightly bitter, tasting of celery. The whole seeds retain their flavour well; crush as needed and use to complement fish and seafood dishes, pickles and relishes, soups, stews, egg dishes, salad dressings, breads and savoury biscuits.

Celeriac, a selected form of *A. graveolens* with a very large taproot, is grown as a root vegetable. It is used raw in salads and cooked in soups and stews.

Celery (*Apium graveolens*)

Chamomile

The flowers of Roman chamomile (*C. nobile*) and German chamomile (*M. recutita*) have been used medicinally since ancient times to treat both skin and digestive disorders.

∙∙

Latin name *Chamaemelum nobile* syn. *Anthemis nobilis* and *Matricaria recutita* Asteraceae
Parts used Flowers, leaves

Roman chamomile (*Chamaemelum nobile*)

🌿 Gardening

Roman or perennial chamomile is a densely carpeting and low-growing plant. Its feathery green leaves have a ripe apple scent and the flowers are single white daisies. It is often confused with German chamomile, an upright growing annual with fine ferny leaves and white daisy flowers. An attractive fully double variety, *C. nobile* 'Flore Plena', is grown commercially for its essential oil in many countries, while a non-flowering variety, *C. nobile* 'Treneague', is popular for lawns. The flowers of dyer's chamomile (*Anthemis tinctoria*) yield a golden brown dye.

• **Growing** All these chamomiles require a sunny position and well-drained soil. Raise from seed in spring.

• **Harvesting and storing** Gather the flowers when fully open. German chamomile will reflower if harvested in summer. Dry, then store in an airtight container.

🌿 Herbal medicine

Matricaria recutita. Part used: flowers. Chamomile's mild sedative effect on the nervous system helps to ease both colic and the pain of menstrual cramps. It can also help to stimulate the digestion and relieve the discomfort of nausea. Chamomile is a gently acting herb, making it especially suitable for children.

Topically, the soothing and anti-inflammatory effects of chamomile are excellent for treating itchy and inflamed skin conditions.

Do not use these herbs in greater than culinary quantities if you are pregnant or breastfeeding.

A multipurpose herb

For a relaxing sleep, try combining the essential oils of both chamomile and lavender in an oil burner. Chamomile is also antifungal and antibacterial. Next time you make chamomile tea, brew a second cup that's extra strong and use the liquid to wipe down the kitchen sink and benches, or to wipe out a cupboard to rid it of a musty smell. Also, spray it onto plants and vegetables to deter fungal diseases such as mildew in the garden.

Roman chamomile (*Chamaemelum nobile*), foreground; German chamomile (*Matricaria recutita*), background

Making an infusion

The word 'infusion' is used to describe a herbal tea or tisane that is made by pouring boiling water over a quantity of fresh or dried herbal material. It is an effective preparation method of extracting water-soluble components from aromatic herbs that contain essential oils, such as chamomile, fennel and peppermint.

1 Place the recommended quantity of loose dried herb (dried chamomile is shown here) or finely chopped fresh herb into a pre-warmed glass or china teapot or coffee plunger.

2 Pour about 200 ml freshly boiled water over the herb and stir. Place the lid on the teapot to trap the steam and prevent the essential oil evaporating. Allow the mixture to steep for 10 to 15 minutes.

3 Stir again before pouring through a strainer into your teacup.

Usage Drink 1 cup of tea 3 times a day over several weeks for chronic (long-standing) problems, or up to 6 cups a day in the shorter term for acute problems.

Storage Infusions do not store well, so it's always best to prepare a fresh pot of tea for each cup.

Every time you make a cup of tea with a tea bag, you are, in fact, making an infusion.

Chervil

This delicious culinary herb, used since Roman times, has a delicate flavour between tarragon and parsley that is indispensable in French cuisine.

....

Latin name *Anthriscus cerefolium* Apiaceae
Also known as Garden chervil
Parts used Leaves, stems

Chervil (*Anthriscus cerefolium*)

Fines herbes

Chervil is especially popular in French cooking, and essential (along with parsley, chives and tarragon) in the classic herb blend called *fines herbes*, which is used fresh with poached fish, shellfish and chicken and in green salads and egg dishes such as omelettes.

🍃 Gardening

Apicius, the renowned gourmet of 1st-century Rome, set his seal of approval on chervil, which is an annual plant with delicate and lacy, fern-like foliage. The tiny white flowers, borne in clusters on slender stems, are followed by thin black seeds.

- **Growing** Chervil requires good drainage and a moist soil that is close to neutral, preferably enriched with compost. Grow chervil in a lightly shaded position, as excessive sun exposure will cause the leaves to burn and turn rose pink. In warm climates, grow chervil in spring, autumn and even winter, as it does have some cold tolerance and will withstand light frosts.

  Scatter seed over the soil, press down lightly and water regularly. Seedlings usually emerge in about 10 to 14 days. Plants are ready for harvesting about 8 to 10 weeks after planting. Chervil has a long taproot and bare-rooted seedlings do not easily transplant. Seed will not germinate in soil that is too warm.

In cool-climate areas with mild summers, grow chervil for a continuous supply during the growing season, although light shade promotes lush growth, and the season can be further extended with the use of protective cloches. Water regularly to promote lush growth.

You can grow chervil as a trap crop to lure slugs away from valued vegetable crops.

• **Harvesting and storing** Harvest leaves before the appearance of flowers and, as with parsley, cut from the outside, preferably with scissors, as the plant is delicate. Leaves are best used fresh, but can also be deep frozen in sealed plastic bags.

Cooking

Chervil flowers, leaves and roots are all edible, although it is the faintly anise-flavoured leaves that are most frequently used. There are various types, including curly leafed varieties that make a pretty garnish.

Use fresh chervil in cooking, as its delicate flavour is destroyed by heat or drying. The herb goes well with glazed carrots and in butter sauces and cream-based soups. Add it at the last minute, after the dish has been taken off the heat and is ready to serve. Chervil frozen into ice cubes adds a refreshing taste to summery fruit drinks.

Chervil butter makes a delicious spread for savoury biscuits or bread and a flavoursome topping for barbecued fish, meat or poultry. Mix chopped chervil with softened butter and lemon juice, form into a log, roll tightly in plastic wrap and chill until required.

Chervil, pea and fetta quiche

4 large eggs
300 ml cream
1/2 teaspoon salt
3 tablespoons roughly chopped fresh chervil
1 tablespoon finely chopped fresh chives
1–2 sheets ready-made shortcrust pastry
1 cup (155 g) fresh shelled peas
120 g soft fetta, crumbled
1/2 cup (60 g) grated cheddar

1 Preheat oven to 180°C. In medium bowl, whisk together eggs and cream; season with salt and stir through herbs.

2 Lightly oil 35 cm x 12 cm rectangular or 23 cm round tin. Place pastry into tin, using 2 sheets if required.

3 Sprinkle top of pastry with peas and fetta. Pour over egg and herb mixture; sprinkle with cheddar.

4 Place quiche on bottom shelf in oven. Bake for 30 to 35 minutes, or until quiche is set. Serve with salad.

SERVES 4

Herb cards and tags

A personalised handmade card is something to treasure, and pressed and dried flowers and herbs are perfect for decorating them.

If you want the cards to last a long time, use acid-free paper, cardboard and cardstock. There is a vast range of beautiful papers and cardstocks available, and many of them are handmade. For example, unryushi paper, handmade in Thailand, is semi-transparent and contains short and long fibres. Mulberry paper comes in a range of textures and thicknesses. It is meant to be torn, not cut, producing a pretty frayed edge. We have given finished measurements but you can adapt them to any size you wish.

Pressed flower wreath card

What you need

This card measures 12 cm square.

☐ 12 x 24 cm pale green cardstock

☐ 12 cm square pale green unryushi or mulberry paper

☐ spray adhesive

☐ deckle-edge scissors

☐ dried herbs and flowers (we used chervil, heartsease and chamomile)

☐ PVA glue

1 Score the pale green cardstock in half crosswise and fold it in half to make a single-fold card.

2 Using deckle-edge scissors, trim the square of unryushi paper to 11 cm.

3 Use spray adhesive to glue the unryushi square to the centre of the card.

4 Arrange dried herbs and flowers into a wreath shape and carefully glue each piece in place.

You can scent your cards with a dab of essential oil or an organza-enclosed insert of fragrant dried flowers (as used in the Valentine card in front).

Herb tags

What you need

This card measures 9 cm square.

☐ 5.5 x 7 cm fine corrugated board

☐ 9 cm square cardstock

☐ 6 x 7 cm plain calico

☐ tacky craft glue

☐ herb sprigs (we used chervil, rosemary, parsley and sage)

☐ hole punch

☐ natural string

1 Glue the corrugated board to the cardboard square on an angle.

2 Fray the edges of the calico a little, then glue it to the centre of the corrugated board, off-setting it again.

3 Glue a sprig of dried herb to the calico background.

4 Punch a hole in one corner and add a string tie.

Chilli

Part of the South American diet for at least 7000 years, chilli varieties are the world's most frequently used spice. The heat is fiercest in the seeds and the white pith.

Latin name *Capsicum* sp. Solanaceae
Part used Fruits

🌿 Gardening

All *Capsicum* species are indigenous to South America. The most commonly grown is *C. annuum*, which contains many chilli varieties as well as the bell peppers, pimentos and other sweet capsicum varieties. Chillies and bell peppers differ from each other by a single gene that produces the fiery-flavoured compound capsaicin.

There are possibly hundreds of named varieties of *C. annuum*, and these have been selected worldwide for climate tolerance, colour, size, shape, degree of heat and flavour, which may vary from citrus and prune to smoky, coffee, raisin, almond and tobacco.

They are all divided into groups by shape: cherry-shaped (Cerasiform), cone-shaped (Coniodes), clustered elongated cones (Fasciculatum), sweet peppers (Grossum) and long hot peppers (Longum).

Among the best known varieties of *C. baccatum* are 'Anaheim', with large, long, tapering, mildly pungent fruit; 'Poblano', which has large, medium-hot, heart-shaped fruits (and is known as 'Ancho' in its dried form); 'Pasilla', a large raisin-flavoured tapering variety; 'Jalapeño', a thick-walled variety which is used in salsas or smoked (when it is known as chipotle); 'Guajillo', a leathery, dark reddish brown variety that is moderately hot; and 'Mirasol', a reselection of a pre-Columbian Mexican variety.

Some — such as 'Purple Tiger', 'Filius Blue' and 'Variegata' syn. 'Bellingrath Gardens' — are ornamental and widely grown for landscape purposes. All are edible as well as being decorative.

The tiny bird peppers — including the wild pepper of New Mexico, the 'Chiltepin' or 'Tepin' — all belong to *C. annuum* var. *aviculare*. 'Tabasco' is the most widely known variety of the species *C. frutescens*.

The species *C. chinense* contains some of the hottest chilli varieties, including the 'Habañero' and its variants, the 'Scotch Bonnet' or 'Jamaican Hot', and the somewhat milder Puerto Rican 'Rocatillo'. All three types are excellent for culinary use and widely grown in the Caribbean. The best known variety, 'Aji Amarillo' or 'Kellu-Uchu', is widely used in the cuisine of Peru.

• **Growing** All chilli varieties require good drainage, full sunshine and an enriched soil. Do not grow chillies where related species of the family Solanaceae, such as tomatoes and eggplants, have recently been grown.

Even the fastest-maturing chilli varieties of *C. annuum* require a minimum growing season of 3 months. In cooler areas, grow seedlings under protection before planting them out after the last frost. Although the fierce heat of the fruit will deter mammal pests, you may need to protect your plants from birds, which are unaffected by the pungent taste.

• **Harvesting and storing** Pick peppers at any time, but remember that they reach peak heat when they turn red. Store fresh chillies in the vegetable drawer of the refrigerator.

The dark purple fruits of Thai chilli (*C. annuum* var. *fasciculatum*) turn bright red when ripe.

🌿 Cooking

It is hard to imagine Indian, West Indian, African and Asian cuisines without chillies, yet they were unknown in those regions until after 1493, when Christopher Columbus brought them back to Europe from the New World. They were then taken to India, Southeast Asia and Africa by Portuguese traders. Today India and China are the largest producers of chillies.

Too hot to handle!

Most of the capsaicin that's responsible for the heat in peppers is stored in the seeds and the white septae within the fruit. To reduce the heat in a dish, you need to remove these before cooking. Capsaicin is not water-soluble, and neither water nor beer will neutralise the heat. It is, however, fat-soluble, and a glass of milk or yogurt, or the Indian yogurt-based drink lassi, are effectively soothing.

Wear protective gloves when chopping quantities of chilli peppers, as they can numb your fingertips for many hours. Also, avoid touching your face, eyes or genitals, in fact anywhere on your bare skin, after preparing them. Do not feed pets food containing chilli, as some breeds can die.

Habañero, a *C. chinense* variety native to Mexico, is among the hottest chillies in common use.

Chillies are always green when unripe; when ripe, they may be red, yellow, purple or almost black. Their heat level varies from negligible to incendiary. In general, the smaller the chilli, the hotter it will be.

Varieties lacking the capsaicin gene produce sweet fruits that taste more like capsicum (to which they are related) and have a fruity flavour but little or no heat. The heat level may vary considerably even among chillies of the same variety, so the stated quantity in a recipe should always be adjusted to taste.

To check the heat level of your chillies, cut the end off one and give it the tiniest, tentative lick. A remedy for chilli burn on the palate is dairy foods, such as milk or yogurt.

To minimise irritation from the fumes when you are grinding chillies, use a spice grinder rather than a mortar and pestle.

Choose firm, shiny fresh chillies; avoid those that are wrinkled. Green chillies are always used fresh; red chillies can be used fresh or dried. Dried chillies differ in flavour to fresh, being fruitier and sweeter, although still retaining their heat. Buy dried chillies whole, crushed or powdered, and fresh chillies whole, or chopped and preserved in vinegar in jars.

Dried chillies: 1. Thai chillies 2. Pasilla 3. Guajillo 4. Habañero 5. Chipotle (dried, smoked jalapeño) 6. Pimentos 7. Ancho (dried poblano).

In one of those transatlantic differences in spelling, 'chilli' — together with the less often used 'chillie' — is used in the United Kingdom (and in Australia), while the Spanish-originated 'chile' is commonly used in the United States and Mexico. The term 'chili' is reserved for a regional hot and spicy stew, originally from Mexico, which the United States subsequently made its own.

Chilli condiments

- **Paprika** is a mildly hot, sweet, bright red chilli powder that is produced by drying and grinding suitable varieties. Spain and Hungary are the world's largest producers. Suitable varieties, which must be intensely red when fully ripened, include 'Hungarian' and 'NuMex Conquistador'.

Cayenne pepper

- **Cayenne** is a powder derived from dried hot red chillies. 'Cayenne' is a pre-Columbian variety from French Guiana.

A number of cayenne-type varieties have been developed from it, including 'Hot Portugal', 'Long Red', 'Ring of Fire' and 'Hades Hot'. Dried chillies and chilli flakes are also used.

- **Tabasco**, the most famous chilli sauce, is made in Louisiana, in the United States, according to a 3-year process invented in 1868 by Edmund McIlhenny.

- **Peri Peri** is a sauce developed by the Portuguese from the tiny but fiery southern African variety 'Peri Peri'; it includes lemons, spices and herbs.

- **Mole poblano** — compounded of chilli (such as pasilla), chocolate, spices and seeds or peanuts — is a popular sauce in Mexico, and increasingly abroad.

Chilli sauces

Chilli and lime sauce

This Caribbean sauce recipe is delicious with barbecued or baked fish or vegetables. Baste the food with it, or serve it separately.

2 fresh red chillies
1 tablespoon salt
1 cup (250 ml) fresh lime juice

1　Remove the seeds and white pith from the chillies if you do not want too much heat. Slice chillies finely and pack into a jar.

2　Dissolve the salt in the lime juice and pour over the chillies. Seal and store in a cool place to let the flavours develop. It is ready for use after 4 days and keeps for up to 4 weeks.

Harissa

This fiery sauce is a feature of North African cooking. Use it as a condiment with eggs and couscous-based dishes. If using fresh chillies, omit the soaking step.

8 dried chillies
2 cloves garlic, peeled
1/2 teaspoon salt
2 tablespoons olive oil
1 teaspoon ground caraway seeds
1 teaspoon ground coriander
1/2 teaspoon ground cumin

1　Soak dried chillies in hot water 30 minutes. Drain. Remove stems and seeds. Place chillies, garlic, salt and olive oil in a food processor; blend to a paste.

2　Add the remaining spices and blend. Pack into an airtight container and top with a thin layer of olive oil. Keeps for a month in the refrigerator. Thin with a little oil and lemon juice or hot stock before using.

Nuoc cham

An indispensable seasoning in Vietnamese cooking, this spicy mixture can be served with mixed salad greens and herbs or as a dipping sauce or marinade.

2 small red chillies, or to taste, seeds removed
2 cloves garlic
1 teaspoon sugar
2 limes, peeled and chopped
1 tablespoon hot water
1 tablespoon vinegar
100 ml fish sauce

1　Pound chillies and garlic to a fine paste. Add sugar and limes, then pound to a pulp.

2　Stir in water, vinegar and fish sauce and serve.

To retain their flavour, store herb vinegars and oils in a cool, dark place.

Herb vinegars

Wine vinegars vary greatly in price and quality, so buy the best you can afford. Use the same method for the seeds of herbs such as dill, fennel, celery and coriander.

....

Tarragon and red wine vinegar

15 fresh tarragon leaves
10 juniper berries
2 cups (500 ml) red wine vinegar

1 Lightly bruise tarragon and berries by hitting them with the flat of a knife. Place bruised leaves and berries in a clean 500 ml bottle; pour in vinegar.

2 Leave 3 to 4 days to allow flavours to develop.

MAKES 2 CUPS (500 ml)

Rice vinegar with coriander

3 fresh lime leaves
4 slices galangal, each 5 mm thick
2 cloves garlic
15–20 fresh coriander leaves
1 cup (250 ml) rice wine vinegar

1 Lightly bruise lime leaves, galangal and garlic by hitting them with the flat of a knife. Place herbs, including coriander leaves, in a clean 250 ml bottle; pour in vinegar.

2 Leave 3 to 4 days to allow flavours to develop.

MAKES 1 CUP (250 ml)

Fennel and saffron vinegar

4 sprigs fresh fennel leaves
2–3 whole dried chillies
2 cloves garlic
1/4 teaspoon fennel seeds
pinch of saffron
2 cups (500 ml) white wine vinegar

1 Place fennel leaves, chillies, garlic, fennel seeds and saffron in a clean 500 ml bottle; pour in vinegar.

2 Leave 3 to 4 days to allow flavours to develop.

MAKES 2 CUPS (500 ml)

Try these, too...

Red chilli vinegar

Cut 1 long red chilli in half lengthwise and place in a clean 750 ml bottle with 2 whole long red chillies. Pour in 3 cups (750 ml) white wine vinegar. Seal and store.

MAKES 3 CUPS (750 ml)

Berry vinegar

Combine 500 g berries (such as a mixture of raspberries, strawberries and blueberries) and 3 cups (750 ml) white wine vinegar in a large ceramic or glass bowl and stir well to lightly bruise fruit. Cover mixture and leave in a cool place for a few days to infuse. Pour mixture into saucepan, bring to the boil and remove from heat. Allow to cool. Strain mixture through a double layer of muslin, into clean jars. Seal and store.

MAKES 3 CUPS (750 ml)

Clove pinks

With an intoxicating spicy fragrance, the pretty flowers of clove pinks resemble small carnations. The fresh petals are edible and are used in salads and desserts.

Latin names *Dianthus caryophyllus* and *D. plumarius* Caryophyllaceae
Also known as Gillyflower
Parts used Petals, whole flowers

 Gardening

Clove pinks were bred from the grass pink or cottage pink (*D. plumarius*) and *D. caryophyllus* (which also gave rise to the carnation). They form a dense, low, spreading cushion of grass-like foliage, from which emerge many flower stems in early summer. All are perennial.

• **Varieties** A remarkable number have survived the centuries, including 'Sops in Wine', used in Elizabethan times to flavour mulled wines. 'Bridal Veil', 'Queen of Sheba', 'Ursula le Grove' and 'Pheasant's Eye' date from the 17th century. Eighteenth-century heirlooms include the Paisley Pinks, such as 'Dad's Favourite' and 'Paisley Gem', which resemble intricate paisley fabric patterning, as well as 'Inchmery' and 'Cockenzie'. Nineteenth-century large double-flowered forms include 'Mrs Sinkins', 'Earl of Essex', 'Rose de Mai' and 'Mrs Gullen'. The Carthusian pink (*D. carthusianorum*) was used in medicinal liqueurs by the Carthusian monks.

The famed Allwoodii 20th-century pinks include 'Arthur', 'Kestor', 'Doris' and 'Fusilier'. Other very fragrant modern pinks include 'Kim Brown', 'Tuscan Lace', 'Highland Fraser', 'Pretty', 'Tudor Manor', 'Jean d'Arc', 'May Queen', 'Falstaff' and 'Gloire Lyonnaise'.

• **Growing** Clove pinks require a well-drained, sunny position. They grow well in pots, and are both drought- and cold-tolerant once established. Pinks thrive in alkaline soil; if gardening on acid soil, add dolomite or garden lime. Alternatively, tuck small pieces of concrete rubble under the plant. These will leak lime into the soil during watering.

Mixed seed of perennial pinks are available. Named varieties must be propagated by cuttings.

• **Harvesting and storing** Harvest flowers as required. To use fresh, remove the bitter white heels of the petals.

Clove pinks (*Dianthus caryophyllus*)

Classic fragrances

Like the spice clove, the flowers of clove pinks and carnations are rich in eugenol, and the perfume absolute is used in many high-quality perfumes, including Floris's 'Malmaison', Nina Ricci's 'L'Air du Temps', Guerlain's 'Samsara' and 'L'Heure Bleu', Worth's 'Je Reviens', Hermès's 'Bel Ami', Estée Lauder's 'White Linen' and Bvlgari's 'Bvlgari for Men'. It takes 500 kg of flowers to produce 100 ml of the essential oil, so synthetics such as eugenol and isoeugenol are often used in modern perfumery.

The Greeks and Romans regarded the clove pink as the flower of the gods.

Comfrey

Comfrey's other common name, knitbone, reflects its traditional use in poultices to aid the healing of broken bones. Comfrey is also a dye and compost accelerator.

Latin name *Symphytum officinale* Boraginaceae
Also known as Knitbone
Parts used Leaves, roots (high in toxic alkaloids)

Gardening

Native to Europe and Asia, common comfrey is a vigorous perennial, with mauve bell-shaped flowers, that grows to about 80 cm. Comfrey is also an 'accumulator', a deep-rooted plant that taps into minerals in the subsoil. A 'soup' made from rotting comfrey leaves in water makes a great organic liquid feed for crops. Other species are the ornamental cream-flowered groundcover *S. grandiflorum*, and *S. asperum*, with bright blue flowers.

Comfrey (*Symphytum officinale*)

The dyer's art

For centuries, dyes have been made from herbs and other plants. Comfrey leaves produce a golden yellow dye, while dandelion roots create a reddish one. Until indigo from the Far East was traded with Europe, woad (*Isatis tinctoria*) was used to produce a blue dye, and the characteristic war paint of the ancient Britons and Celts was made from it. In today's commercial world, synthetic dyes are favoured over natural ones because they are resistant to fading from exposure to light. To make your own herbal dyes, consult the internet or craft books.

- **Growing** Comfrey grows readily from segments of root and, once established, is difficult to remove. It prefers full sun but can tolerate partial shade. Dig the site deeply, space segments of root 1 m apart and cover with about 5 cm of soil. An annual top dressing of rotted manure is recommended. Water regularly in the first season. Comfrey can also be grown from seed sown in spring or autumn.
- **Harvesting and storing** Harvest mature plants up to 5 times a year. Cut with shears and wear protective gloves, as the hairs on the leaves are an irritant. Leaves can be dried flat on racks. Do not harvest in the first year or after early autumn. Make sure you leave some root in the ground for the following year's growth.

🍃 Herbal medicine

Symphytum officinale. Parts used: leaves, roots. Comfrey has long been an important part of the herbal medicine chest, used traditionally as a topical application for bruises, fractures and wounds. It has a remarkable reputation for hastening the repair and renewal of damaged tissue as well as reducing inflammation. One of the compounds found in comfrey, called allantoin and thought to be responsible for many of the healing effects of this herb, has been shown to have a regenerative action on connective tissue. To use, blend juice extracted from fresh leaves into a cream and apply topically, or make a poultice (see below).

Do not use comfrey internally as it contains compounds that are potentially toxic. Do not use comfrey if you are pregnant or breastfeeding.

The Romans called comfrey *conferva*, which means 'join together'.

Making a poultice

A poultice is a topical application of a fresh herb, which is used to encourage healing of injured muscles and bones (for example, strains, sprains and fractures), or to draw matter out of the skin.

1   Chop sufficient fresh herb to cover the affected body part. Place in a container and blend using a stick blender, adding a little water if necessary. The finished mixture should be of a mushy consistency.

2   Place the mixture on a piece of folded muslin. Use a spatula or the back of a spoon to spread the mixture thinly so that the surface area will cover the whole area of the affected body part.

3   Rub a little body oil onto the affected body part to prevent the poultice sticking to the skin. Apply the poultice, covering the muslin with plastic wrap to keep it in place. To make it more secure, if necessary, place a bandage around the poultice.

Usage Change the poultice about every couple of hours, or, if possible, leave it in place overnight.

Coriander

Coriander's fragrant foliage, roots and seeds were widely used in the ancient world for medicinal as well as culinary purposes. It was also a favourite of medieval herbalists.

Latin name *Coriandrum sativum* Apiaceae
Also known as Chinese parsley, cilantro
Parts used Leaves, seeds, roots

Coriander (*Coriandrum sativum*)

Coriander and figs

Palathai, or fig cakes, date from Roman times. They are popular in Egypt and Turkey. Remove stalks from 400 g dried figs (select soft ones). Process figs to a paste in food processor. Shape into an oval cake with your hands. Combine 1 teaspoon freshly ground coriander seeds and 1 teaspoon flour. Dust cake with mixture. Serve wedges for dessert.

🌿 Gardening

Native to northern Africa and western Asia, coriander's long history of cultivation goes back to the time of the ancient Egyptians. It was found in the tombs of pharaohs, is mentioned in the Bible and is one of the bitter herbs traditionally eaten at Passover. The herb reached Britain with the Romans, and was one of the plants taken to North America by the early colonists.

An annual, coriander resembles flat-leaf parsley, although it is more tender in texture. The leaves are dissected into wedge-shaped segments, developing a fern-like appearance. Vietnamese coriander or rau ram (*Polygonum odoratum*) is a leafy perennial used in tropical areas. The leaves of Mexican coriander or culantro (*Eryngium foetidum*) are strongly aromatic.

• **Growing** Coriander prefers a sunny position. Sow directly in the garden in spring after the last frost. You can assist the germination process by rubbing the seed, separating it into halves and then presoaking the halved seeds for 48 hours. Coriander will grow well in either garden beds or pots.

• **Harvesting and storing** Harvest the seed crop when half the seeds on the plant have turned brown. Tie harvested stems into bunches and then hang them upside-down inside paper bags to trap the falling seed. Once the plant is full size, harvest young foliage to use fresh at any time.

Herbal medicine

Coriandrum sativum. Part used: dried ripe fruits (seeds). The volatile oils in coriander seeds have antispasmodic properties and a stimulating effect on the appetite and can be chewed to help relieve minor digestive complaints.

Traditionally, coriander is often used in conjunction with caraway, fennel, cardamom and anise to ease symptoms of indigestion, including spasm, flatulence, and abdominal distension.

For the safe and appropriate medicinal use of coriander, consult your healthcare professional. Do not use coriander in greater than culinary quantities if you are pregnant or breastfeeding.

Cooking

The pungent leaves and stalks are popular in Southeast Asian, Middle Eastern, Mediterranean, African, South American and Mexican cooking, in salads, soups, legume dishes, salsas, curries and stir-fries. In India, the leaf is used in types of fresh chutneys. Long cooking destroys the flavour of the leaves, so use them raw or add just before serving.

Roast the seeds to enhance their flavour. Used whole or ground, their mild, slightly sweet taste works well in sweet and savoury dishes and in sauces such as harissa (see recipe *page 47*). The fibre in ground seeds absorbs liquid and helps to thicken curries and stews.

The root has a more intense flavour than leaves. It is used in Thai cooking, especially pounded into curry pastes.

Coriander and chilli butter

¼ cup (40 g) macadamia nuts, roughly chopped
250 g butter, softened
3 tablespoons roughly chopped fresh coriander leaves
2 fresh lime leaves, finely chopped
1 large red chilli, finely diced
1 tablespoon lime juice

1 Toast chopped macadamia nuts in a dry frying pan over medium heat, tossing until smallest pieces are just golden. Transfer to small bowl; cool before use.

2 Place softened butter in medium bowl. Add toasted nuts and remaining ingredients; mix until well combined.

3 Place mixture on a piece of plastic wrap about 20 cm long. Roll mixture into a log about 5 cm in diameter; wrap tightly. Chill until required.

Vegetarian spring rolls

50 g vermicelli

12 medium round rice paper wrappers

2 Lebanese or small cucumbers, seeded
   and cut into thin strips

4 spring onions, trimmed

1 red capsicum, cut into strips

12 snow peas, cut into strips

1 carrot, cut into strips

12 fresh mint leaves

12 fresh coriander leaves

12 fresh basil leaves

Dipping sauce

2 tablespoons lime juice

1 tablespoon fish sauce

1 teaspoon sugar

1 small red chilli, seeded and finely sliced

1   Place vermicelli in heatproof medium bowl and cover
   with boiling water. Stand 10 to 15 minutes, or until
   soft; drain and set aside.

2   Place rice paper rounds in medium bowl of warm
   water until just softened (about 30 seconds).
   Carefully lay each one out flat on work surface or
   cutting board and gently pat dry with paper towel.

3   Divide vermicelli, vegetables and herbs among the
   rice paper rounds, placing them in the centre of each

one. Fold in the edges of the wrapper and roll into
a cigar shape.

4   To make dipping sauce, combine all ingredients in
   medium bowl; stir to dissolve sugar. Serve in a small
   bowl with rolls.

SERVES 4

Folding the rolls

Place vegetable mixture in centre
of the rice paper wrapper.

Fold in one side of the round and
then two opposing sides.

Roll into a compact cigar shape
to enclose filling.

Curry plant

The intensely silvered needle-like foliage of this plant releases a mouth-watering fragrance of curry. The flowers can be dried and included in floral arrangements.

....

Latin name *Helichrysum italicum* syn.
H. angustifolium Asteraceae
Also known as Italian everlasting
Parts used Leaves, flowers

Gardening

The common form of curry plant found in herb gardens is *H. italicum* subsp. *italicum*, a form widely sold in the nursery trade as *H. angustifolium*. It is an upright but eventually semi-sprawling shrub to about 60 cm, with dense, needle-shaped leaves covered in very fine hairs, which give the plant a silvered appearance.
• **Growing** Curry plant requires an open sunny position and a very well-drained soil. In areas where the temperature can drop below –5°C, grow plants under protection in winter. The plant is affected by prolonged rain, often developing fungus on the foliage. To avoid this, mulch around the plant with gravel and ensure the plant has excellent air circulation.
• **Harvesting and storing** As a herb, curry plant is only used fresh. Pick sprigs as required.

Cooking

The entire plant is strongly aromatic of curry, particularly after rain. Add sprigs to egg, rice and vegetable dishes to impart a mild curry flavour, but cook only briefly.

Curry plant responds well to trimming, so consider using it in a low-growing, aromatic hedge.

Curry tree

Curry plant is sometimes confused with the curry tree (*Murraya koenigii*), which is used in Ayurvedic medicine. This small tree with pinnate leaves is also intensely curry-scented and may eventually reach 3 to 4 m. Use fresh leaves in Indian dishes, adding them just before serving. The curry tree makes an attractive container plant, preferring a warm climate in full sun to partial shade.

Curry plant (*Helichrysum italicum*)

Dandelion

Dandelions are the plant world's equivalent of the pig: almost all of it is eaten. Young leaves are used in cooking, the flowers to make wine and the roots for herbal coffee.

. . . .

Latin name *Taraxacum officinale* Asteraceae
Also known as Clocks and watches, fairy clocks
Parts used Leaves, roots, flowers

Dandelion flowers are rich in pollen and nectar, attracting beneficial insects such as bees to the garden.

🍃 Gardening

Dandelion is a perennial with a thick, fleshy taproot and coarsely toothed leaves. The golden yellow flowers are followed by spherical balls of seed, or 'clocks', which are dispersed by the wind.

- **Growing** Dandelion requires a sunny situation. Sow the seed directly into the soil in spring.
- **Harvesting and storing** Blanch the leaves for culinary purposes by covering them from the light for 2 to 3 weeks before harvesting in late spring and before flowering occurs. Lift roots at the end of the second season. Both leaves and roots can be dried for herbal use.

🍃 Cooking

The dandelion variety 'Thick Leaved' has leaves that can be used fresh in salads, or cooked like spinach.

Dandelion and burdock is a traditional British, naturally fizzy soft drink made from fermented dandelion and burdock roots — in much the same way as root beer and sarsaparilla.

Clock flower

Dandelion has acquired a number of names, including *piss en lit* (French for 'wet the bed'), alluding to its diuretic effect, while its English name comes from *dent de lion* (French for 'lion's tooth'), a reference to its toothed leaves. Other common names include fairy clocks and clocks and watches, both of which refer to the children's game of telling time by the number of seeds left after blowing a 'clock'. Another name, *caput monachi*, refers to the tonsured head of a medieval monk.

Dandelion (*Taraxacum officinale*)

Cleansing cures

Because of its powerful diuretic action dandelion leaf is traditionally regarded as one of the most important herbal remedies for the elimination of excess fluid. The bitter-tasting root, taken as an infusion, stimulates gastrointestinal function and is traditionally used for minor digestive ailments, especially sluggish liver and gall bladder function, indigestion and mild cases of constipation. Do not use dandelion in greater than culinary quantities if you are pregnant or breastfeeding.

Dandelion root infusion

An infusion of roasted dandelion root is a popular caffeine-free alternative to coffee and a pleasant way to stimulate digestion before or after a heavy meal.

Infuse ½ to 2 teaspoons (2 to 8 g) dried or roasted dandelion root in boiling water. Drink 3 cups per day.

If using the roasted root, add milk or soy milk to taste, but avoid sweeteners, as they may diminish the herb's effectiveness.

Detox tea

The humble dandelion is a powerful detoxification agent, helping rid the body of waste. Red clover and alfalfa are traditional digestive and kidney tonics.

2 teaspoons dried dandelion
1 teaspoon dried red clover
1 teaspoon dried alfalfa
1 teaspoon lemon zest
2 cups (500 ml) boiling water

Place herbs in a teapot and pour in boiling water. Cover pot and steep for 15 minutes; strain. Drink 2 to 3 cups per day.

Dandelion leaf tea

Dandelion tea may help reduce fluid retention and assist the removal of toxins from the body.

Infuse 1 to 2 teaspoons (4 to 10 g) of dried dandelion leaf in boiling water. Drink 3 cups per day.

A good garden may have some weeds.

A proverb

Dill

Traditionally, if you suffered from hiccups, insomnia or indigestion, dill was an ideal remedy. Its name comes from the old Norse word 'dylla', meaning 'to soothe' or 'lull'.

Latin name *Anethum graveolens* Apiaceae
Also known as Dillweed
Parts used Leaves, seeds

Gather seedheads in summer to dry for use in cooking and medicinal infusions.

🍃 Gardening

Dill is an annual plant with feathery, aromatic, blue-green foliage and attractive flat-headed clusters of yellow flowers, which are followed by small elliptical flat seeds.

Dill varieties suited to dillweed harvesting that are also slow to bolt include 'Hercules', 'Tetra Leaf' and 'Dukat', which is strongly flavoured. Dwarf varieties suited to pot culture include 'Fernleaf' and 'Bouquet'.

Dill (*Anethum graveolens*)

If you are growing dill for seed, 'Long Island Mammoth' is a good dual-purpose heirloom variety.

● **Growing** Dill requires full sun and a well-drained, moist soil. Sow seeds directly into the soil in spring after the last frost, lightly cover them with soil and keep them moist until they germinate, or plant seedlings with the potting soil attached. You may need to stake some tall varieties. Thin plants to 45 cm apart.

● **Harvesting and storing** Harvest leaves as required. Spread them thinly on paper, then microwave them to retain good colour and fragrance. Store in an airtight container in a cool, dry place. Store fresh leaves in a plastic bag in the refrigerator, or chop them finely, put into ice-cube trays, top up with water and freeze. Harvest the seeds after the heads have dried on the plant.

🍃 Herbal medicine

Anethum graveolens. Part used: dried ripe fruits (seeds). The essential oil found in dill seed is a key ingredient in dill water (commonly known as gripe water), a popular treatment for flatulence and intestinal colic in infants and children. The herb's essential oil acts as an antispasmodic, with the effect of releasing wind and reducing pain and discomfort. Dill seeds have also been used to improve the flow of breast milk in breastfeeding mothers. Dill seeds can be used in adults for digestive disorders characterised by wind, bloating and cramping.

To take, grind up to 2 teaspoons (4 g) dill seeds to release the essential oil before infusing them in boiling water. Drink up to 3 cups per day to relieve bloating and flatulence in yourself or colic in a breastfed baby. Used in this way, even culinary quantities of dill seeds can allow the herb's medicinal properties to be passed on to the child. For babies over the age of 3 months, allow the infusion to cool and give 1 to 3 teaspoons at a time up to 4 times a day.

Do not use dill in greater than culinary quantities if you are pregnant or breastfeeding.

Cooking

With a taste reminiscent of anise and parsley, the fresh leaves complement soft cheeses, sour cream, white sauces, egg dishes, seafood and chicken, salads, soups and vegetables dishes, especially potatoes. Dill is famously used in gravlax, a Scandinavian dish of salmon cured with salt and dill.

Add fresh dill to hot dishes just before serving, as cooking dulls its flavour. Conversely, heat brings the flavour in dill seeds, which are often roasted before use.

Dill seeds are used in pickling spice mixtures, in the Moroccan spice mix ras el hanout, in breads (especially rye bread), and in commercial seasonings for meat.

Savoury dill and caraway scones

2 cups (300 g) plain flour
1 tablespoon sugar
1 tablespoon onion powder
1 tablespoon snipped fresh dill
2 teaspoons caraway seeds, plus extra for sprinkling (optional)
1 teaspoon baking powder
3/4 teaspoon salt
1/2 teaspoon bicarbonate of soda
1/2 teaspoon coarsely ground black pepper
120 g butter, chilled
1 egg yolk
3/4 cup (185 g) sour cream
1/2 cup (125 g) ricotta
1 tablespoon thick cream

1 Preheat the oven to 200°C. Grease two baking trays.

2 In a large bowl, combine the flour, sugar, onion powder, dill, caraway seeds, baking powder, salt, bicarbonate of soda and pepper. Using a blunt-ended knife or a pastry cutter, cut in the butter until the mixture resembles coarse crumbs.

3 Combine the egg yolk, sour cream and ricotta, then stir into the crumb mixture until just moistened. Turn onto a floured surface and knead gently 10 times.

4 Pat the dough into two 15 cm circles. Cut each into six wedges. Separate the wedges and place on the prepared baking trays. Brush the tops with cream and sprinkle with additional caraway seeds if you like. Bake for 15 to 8 minutes, or until golden brown. Serve warm.

MAKES 12

Echinacea

Long valued as a medicinal herb used in the prevention and cure of the common cold, echinacea is also a strikingly handsome plant that attracts butterflies to the garden.

....

Latin name *Echinacea* sp. Asteraceae
Also known as Coneflower
Parts used Roots, leaves, flowers, seed

Gardening

There are nine species of echinacea, all North American, of which three are commonly used medicinally.

Echinacea purpurea syn. *Rudbeckia purpurea* is the best known and the most widely grown species. Its roots are the most potent part of the plant, but the leaves and seeds are also used in herbal medicine. A number of varieties are valued as ornamentals and as cut flowers while retaining their herbal potency. They include 'Magnus', with rose-purple flowers; 'White Swan', which is believed to have a similar potency to the pink forms; and the large-flowered 'Primadonna' series, available in deep rose

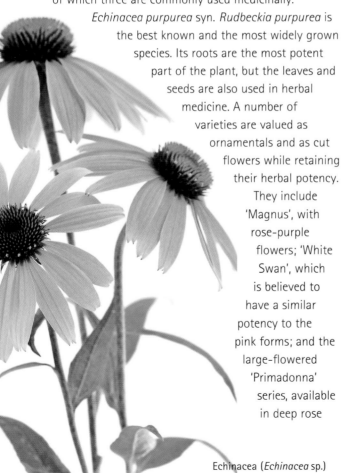

Echinacea (*Echinacea* sp.)

and pure white. Narrowleaf echinacea (*E. angustifolia*) and pale purple echinacea (*E. pallida*) are more potent medicinally than *E. purpurea*. Yellow echinacea or yellow coneflower (*E. paradoxa*) is a handsome species that has large flowers with yellow petals and a chocolate centre.

• **Growing** Echinaceas require a well-drained, sunny position. The plants are deep-rooted and, if grown in areas with shallow soil, should be planted into raised beds. They are drought resistant once they are established. Echinaceas are perennials, and can be divided in autumn and spring or propagated by root cuttings. However, most propagation is by seed, which will germinate more readily after stratification (see box on opposite page).

• **Harvesting and storing** Dig up the roots of mature plants in autumn, then clean and dry them. Gather flowers and foliage from mature plants as required.

Herbal medicine

Echinacea angustifolia, E. purpurea, E. pallida. Parts used: roots, aerial parts. Echinacea was widely used by Native Americans and early colonists to treat colds, flu and acute upper respiratory infections. Its use declined with the development of antibacterial medications but

Echinacea takes its name from the Greek *echinos*, meaning hedgehog, a reference its spiky seedheads.

in the 1990s it returned to favour as a cure for the common cold. Although a number of clinical trials threw doubt on its efficacy, a 2007 review of these results concluded that taking echinacea regularly through the cold season can decrease the likelihood of getting a cold by 50 per cent, and that if a cold did occur, it shortened the duration of the condition.

The most appropriate dose of echinacea depends on both the plant part and the species used, but it is important to start taking the herb as soon as possible after symptoms develop. Preparations made from the root of *Echinacea angustifolia* or *E. pallida* are generally taken at doses of about 1 g taken 3 times daily to treat colds or, in lower doses, as a preventative.

For *E. purpurea*, either the whole plant (including roots) or the aerial parts may be used. The dose is up to 2 g taken 3 times daily as an infusion of dried herb, or 3 ml juice made from the fresh plant and taken 3 times daily.

To make the juice, liquefy fresh aerial parts of *E. purpurea* with a little water in a home juicer or stick blender. The juice doesn't store well, so make only as much as you need to use immediately.

Do not take echinacea if you are pregnant or if you are breastfeeding.

Stratifying seed

To speed germination, stratify your seeds. Mix seed with moist sterile sand or vermiculite and place in a sealed plastic bag in the crisper section of the refrigerator for 4 weeks. Plant treated seed into pots. Transplant into the ground once the roots have filled the pots.

Elder

So strong is the continuing belief in the mystical and magical powers of the elder, that many people ask the tree's permission before harvesting its flowers or berries.

....

Latin name *Sambucus nigra* Caprifoliaceae
Also known as Bore tree, devil's wood, Frau Holle, Judas tree, pipe tree
Parts used Flowers, ripe berries, leaves (for insecticidal purposes only)

Elder (*Sambucus nigra*)

🍃 Gardening

The European or common elder is a deciduous, multi-stemmed shrub–tree with deep green leaves that repel flies, mosquitoes and midgets. It bears lacy, flat-topped clusters of tiny, creamy white, fragrant flowers.

The leaves, bark, green berries and roots are poisonous if consumed.

Ripe elderberries are the nutritional equal of grapes.

• **Growing** These cold-hardy plants prefer a moist but well-drained, humus-rich soil and full sun to partial shade. Take advantage of elder's insecticidal properties by making a strong infusion of elder leaves and use it to repel aphids, mites, leafhoppers, cabbage loopers and whitefly from the garden.

• **Harvesting and storing** Harvest the berries when they are black and fully ripe. Gather open flowers early on a dewless morning, spread the heads on clean kitchen paper and leave in a warm, dark dry place for several days. Strip off flowers when dry.

🍃 Herbal medicine

Sambucus nigra. Parts used: flowers, berries.
Elderflowers and berries have a long history of use for alleviating the symptoms of colds and flu, in particular congestion of the nose and sinuses. Elderflowers have also been used to reduce mucus production in hay fever, sinusitis and middle ear infections.
Recently, clinical trials found that a commercial elderberry syrup reduced both the symptoms and duration of flu in

The young stems, with the poisonous pith removed, were once used to make flutes.

sufferers. Laboratory studies suggest that constituents in the berries may activate certain immune cells and act directly on viruses to reduce their infectivity.

Do not use elder in greater than culinary quantities if you are pregnant or breastfeeding.

Cooking

Use the fresh flowers to brew elderflower 'champagne', a refreshing, non-alcoholic summertime drink, or to make elderflower cordial or a herbal infusion; such processing results in a pleasant floral-tasting beverage. Fresh elderflowers can also be used to flavour stewed fruits, jellies and jams.

High in vitamins A and C, the juice of the ripe berries is fermented to produce elderberry wine or boiled with sugar to make elderberry cordial.

Fresh ripe berries can be made into jam, jelly, chutney and sauces, and cooked as filling for tarts. You can freeze the berries for later use, but cook them for a few minutes first and use them in baked goods.

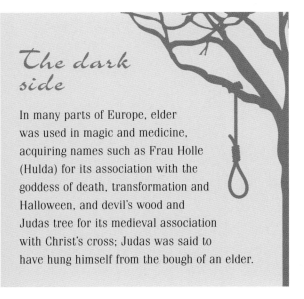

The dark side

In many parts of Europe, elder was used in magic and medicine, acquiring names such as Frau Holle (Hulda) for its association with the goddess of death, transformation and Halloween, and devil's wood and Judas tree for its medieval association with Christ's cross; Judas was said to have hung himself from the bough of an elder.

Elderberry and blackberry jam

750 g elderberries (prepared weight)
150–200 ml water
750 g blackberries, hulled and rinsed
1.5 kg sugar

1 Strip elderberries off stalk; pick over and discard any shrivelled fruit. Wash and drain carefully. Simmer in the water until soft and pulpy. Rub through a sieve to remove seeds.

2 Return elderberry pulp to the saucepan, add blackberries, and simmer for 10 minutes or until soft.

3 Add sugar and stir until dissolved. Increase the heat and boil rapidly until setting point is reached.

4 Spoon into warm, sterilised jars and seal.

MAKES 8 250 ml JARS

Eucalyptus

Eucalypts are rich in essential oils that are valued for both their medicinal applications and their fragrance, which ranges from lemon to peppermint and turpentine.

....

Latin names *Eucalyptus* sp., *Corymbia* sp.
Myrtaceae
Also known as Gum tree
Parts used Leaves, gum (kino)

Gardening

The genus *Eucalyptus*, largely indigenous to Australia, consists of a diverse range of flowering trees and shrubs.

Kino, a gum produced as a response to wounding of the tree, is gathered commercially from species such as scribbly gum, also known as white gum kino (*E. haemostoma*). Many species are steam-distilled for their essential oil. These include the lemon-scented gum (*Corymbia citriodora* syn. *Eucalyptus citriodora*) and lemon ironbark (*E. staigeriana*), which has a fragrance of lemon and rosemary, and *E. globulus*, the most significant species. Narrow-leafed peppermint (*E. radiata*) yields a sweet, fruity essential oil with some camphor. The commercial chemotype of broad-leafed peppermint (*E. dives*) produces a pepperminty essential oil with sweet balsamic notes; it is used in toiletries and aromatherapy. Gully gum (*E. smithii*) essential oil is used in aromatherapy.

Some eucalyptus species have shown weedy tendencies in parts of the world, such as South Africa, so consult local plant services before growing them.

• **Growing** Most species require a sunny position and a well-drained soil. In general, they do not tolerate low temperatures and are quite drought-tolerant once established. When mature, they are able to regenerate after fire. Plantation-grown crops are usually coppiced

Eucalyptus sp.

for ease of harvesting and to improve yields. The oils in eucalypt leaves render them distasteful to most insects.

• **Harvesting and storing** The foliage of mature or regenerated coppiced trees is harvested for steam distillation.

Herbal medicine

Eucalyptus globulus. Part used: leaves.

The essential oil from eucalyptus leaves possesses significant antibacterial and antiviral effects, making it a popular remedy for upper respiratory tract infections, predominantly as a decongestant for catarrhal conditions.

It is commonly used as an external preparation in the form of a chest rub or as an inhalant with a few drops added to a vaporiser or put on a handkerchief. Internal use of the essential oil is not recommended except in commercial preparations, such as cough lozenges, in which the oil is present in a diluted form.

Topical uses of the oil include as a cold sore treatment. It is also an ingredient in a number of ointments used to relieve muscle aches and joint pain.

For the safe and appropriate use of eucalyptus, consult your healthcare professional. Do not use eucalyptus if you are pregnant or breastfeeding.

Chewing gum

Contrary to popular belief, the drowsy koala is not permanently intoxicated from ingesting eucalyptus oil. The real reason that koalas sleep for up to 20 hours a day is because the low-nutrient gum leaves that form the major part of their diet require a great deal of digesting and give them little energy.

Multi-tasking household helper

With its powerful natural antiseptic, disinfectant and cleaning properties, eucalyptus oil can be put to work in every room of the house.

Eucalyptus floor wash

This simple solution can be used on both timber and lino floors. When washing a timber floor, remember not to saturate it. Your mop should be damp, not dripping wet, and the floor should be well-swept or vacuumed before mopping.

1 teaspoon eucalyptus oil
2 tablespoons methylated spirits
5 litres hot water (about half a bucket)

1   Combine all the ingredients in a bucket.

2   Wring out a mop in the solution and use it to damp mop the floor. Leave to dry; you don't need to rinse.

Super stain remover

Eucalyptus oil is invaluable for removing stains – particularly grease and perspiration – from clothing and other fabric. Moisten a clean rag with a little oil and dab the stain from the edge to the middle, then launder as usual.

You can also use it to remove scuff marks and sticky spills from all types of hard floor.

Use a little eucalyptus oil on a cotton pad to remove a stubborn label and glue from a jar.

Eucalyptus wool wash

For generations this recipe has been used to wash woollen garments. It's ideal for blankets, quilts and pillows, too. The eucalyptus helps to keep the wool soft and repels moths. There is no need to rinse it out unless you are washing white items, in which case rinsing will prevent yellowing.

2 cups (500 ml) water
2 cups (200 g) pure soap flakes
½ cup (125 ml) methylated spirits
2½ teaspoons eucalyptus oil

1   Bring the water to the boil and stir in the soap flakes. Remove the pan from the heat and continue to stir until the soap has dissolved and the mixture is smooth.

2   Add the methylated spirits and the eucalyptus oil and mix well.

3   Spoon the mixture into a wide-mouthed jar, where it will set fairly solid.

4   To use the wool wash, dissolve 1 to 2 tablespoons in a bucket of warm water. Keep the unused mixture tightly sealed.

Evening primrose

Evening primroses gain their name from the many species that are pollinated by moths, opening their flowers at night and pouring forth exquisite fragrance.

....

Latin name *Oenothera* sp. Onagraceae
Also known as Suncups, sundrops
Parts used Seeds, roots, leaves

Evening primrose (*Oenothera biennis*)

🌿 Gardening

The principal species cultivated for evening primrose oil extraction is *O. biennis*, a tall biennial which bears clusters of buds that open during successive nights. The large, circular, faintly phosphorescent lemon-coloured flowers mimic the moon and, together with their sweet lemon and tuberose fragrance, attract moths, their chief pollinators. By the following morning, the flowers begin to wither and turn reddish orange, later developing slender pods, which are filled with tiny seed.

• **Growing** Wild *Oenothera* species require a sunny position and are very tolerant of poor soils. Sow seed in spring to early summer. Extreme heat in summer reduces the gamma-linolenic content.

• **Harvesting and storing** Gather the fresh young leaves as required. Lift roots at the end of the second season and use them as a vegetable. Gather the seed when ripe; shattering can be a problem.

🌿 Herbal medicine

Oenothera biennis. Part used: seed oil. Evening primrose oil (EPO) contains significant levels of omega-6 essential fatty acids, especially gamma-linolenic acid (GLA), thought to be involved in many of the oil's therapeutic effects. GLA has notable anti-inflammatory activity and several clinical studies suggest that this effect may be

of benefit in alleviating the symptoms of diabetes-related nerve damage and eczema.

Further trials also indicate that EPO may help to reduce breast tenderness that occurs in the second half of the menstrual cycle and to ease the discomfort of dry eyes. The latest research suggests that a greater therapeutic effect may be achieved if EPO or GLA supplements are taken in combination with omega-3 essential fatty acids, found in flax seeds and fish.

For the safe and effective use of EPO, consult your healthcare professional. Do not use EPO if you are pregnant or breastfeeding.

Evening primrose oil tends to be taken in high doses; capsules, available in health food stores and on prescription, are the most convenient method.

Just-cut herbs add extra zing to your cooking and boost the refreshing flavour of herbal teas.

Eyebright

Eyebright is a European alpine wildflower that takes its common name from its use in eye ailments, including conjunctivitis, styes and the inflammation caused by hay fever.

. . . .

Latin name *Euphrasia officinalis* Orobanchaceae
Parts used Whole plant

Eyebright (*Euphrasia officinalis*)

🍃 Gardening

The use of eyebright dates back to the Middle Ages when it was cultivated in Northern European monastic herb gardens. All *Euphrasia* species are semi-parasitic on the roots of host plants, particularly meadowland grasses, including plantain (*Plantago* sp.) and clover (*Trifolium* sp.). The main species used herbally are *E. officinalis*, *E. brevipila* and *E. rostkoviana*, all annual herbs with yellow-throated white flowers, striped or spotted with purple.

• **Growing** Eyebright's native habitat is cool climate meadowland with alkaline soil and if you have these conditions, simply scatter seed around host grasses during spring. If growing seedlings in pots, add dolomite or lime to the soil and also some established soft meadow grasses. Ensure that the soil remains moist.

• **Harvesting** Harvest the whole plant when in flower, and dry it for use in herbal preparations.

🍃 Herbal medicine

Euphrasia officinalis. Parts used: leaves, flowers. Eyebright has traditionally been used as a remedy for irritated or inflamed conditions of the eye. To refresh eyes that are tired or aggravated by dust, dip a clean cloth into chilled infusion made of dried eyebright, and place over eyes. Rest for 10 minutes. Eyebright can also ease many of the symptoms of hay fever, including itchy, weeping eyes, watery secretions of the nose and also sinus headaches. Infuse up to 1 teaspoon of dried eyebright in boiling water; drink 3 cups per day.

For the safe and effective use of eyebright, consult your healthcare professional. Do not use eyebright if you are pregnant or breastfeeding.

Reading a plant's divine sign

Eyebright was first recorded as a medicinal herb for 'all evils of the eye' in the 14th century. Faith in its use was strengthened by the *Doctrine of Signatures*, a philosophy propounded in the 16th century by a Swiss physician who adopted the name Paracelsus. He proposed that, by observation of a plant's colour and form, or the place where it grew, one could determine its purpose in God's plan. The purple and yellow spots and stripes on eyebright's pale petals were thought to resemble such eye ailments as bloodshot eyes. Hence, it could be used to treat such disorders and infections.

Fennel

Because of fennel's value as a vegetable, flavouring and ornamental plant, it is little wonder that emperor Charlemagne decreed it be grown in every monastery garden.

•••

Latin name *Foeniculum vulgare* Apiaceae
Parts used Leaves, flowers, seeds, stems, roots

🍃 Gardening

Fennel plants are annual or perennial and can reach 1.5 m or more, with one to several erect, hollow stems coming from the base and bearing fine, glossy aromatic

Fennel (*Foeniculum vulgare*)

pinnate foliage. The tiny yellow flowers are used in pickling and the small seeds are very aromatic.

There are two subspecies: a large group classified under *F. vulgare* subsp. *vulgare*, which contains the annual Florence fennel, with its enlarged bulbous leaf bases grown as a vegetable; and the second, *F. vulgare* subsp. *piperitum*, consisting of only the pepper or Italian fennel.

• **Growing** Fennel prefers a light, well-drained soil in a sunny position but is adaptable and tolerates the cold well. Raise all fennel varieties by seed sown in spring. Propagate perennial forms by division in spring.

• **Harvesting and storing** Harvest foliage and flowers as required. Harvest seeds when ripe, then dry and freeze for a few days to kill any insects. Lift roots in autumn and dry them.

🍃 Herbal medicine

Foeniculum vulgare. Part used: dried ripe fruits (seeds). Fennel has calming effects on the digestive system, relieving flatulence, bloating and abdominal discomfort, and its pleasant taste and gentle action make it popular for such conditions in children. Fennel has also

The bulbous leaf bases of Florence fennel are delicious sliced raw in salads or roasted.

been taken by breastfeeding mothers as a remedy for improving breast milk flow; used in this way, the therapeutic effects of fennel can be passed on to breastfed infants experiencing colic and griping.

Fennel has long been used to treat respiratory complaints with catarrh and coughing, and is suitable for treating these conditions in adults and children.

For the safe and appropriate medicinal use of fennel, consult your healthcare professional. Do not use fennel in greater than culinary doses if you are pregnant or breastfeeding except on medical advice.

Around the home

Fennel is a natural flea repellent. Crush a handful of fresh fronds and rub them all over your dog or cat. Put handfuls of fennel fronds under your pet's bedding.

Cooking

Slice the raw bulb thinly and add to salads, or cut in half and roast as a vegetable to bring out its sweetness.

Use fresh fennel leaves in salads, salad dressings and vinegars, with fish, pork and seafood dishes, or as a garnish. The dried seeds are used in cakes and breads, Italian sausages, salads, pickles, curries and pasta and tomato dishes.

Field of Marathon

The ancient Greek name for fennel, *marathon*, was also the name of the battlefield to the north of Athens where, in 490 BCE, a Greek army defeated the invading Persian force. Word of the Greek victory was carried the 42 km to Athens from the battlefield by a runner, who died on the spot after delivering his message.

Crushed potatoes flavoured with fennel seeds

8 unpeeled small baking (floury) potatoes
  (about 750 g in total)
3 tablespoons garlic-infused olive oil
2 teaspoons fennel seeds
1 teaspoon sea salt
1 teaspoon grated lemon zest
1 tablespoon finely chopped fresh parsley

1 Preheat the oven to 240°C. Scrub the potatoes and cook in a saucepan of boiling water for 10 to 15 minutes, until tender. Drain well. Place on a baking tray lined with baking paper.

2 Crush each potato using a potato masher. Drizzle with the oil and sprinkle with remaining ingredients. Bake for 30 minutes, until golden and crunchy.

SERVES 4

Feverfew

With a long history in European herbal medicine, the name feverfew is derived from 'febrifuge', as it was said to dispel fevers. It is also an insect repellent.

The strong-smelling leaves of feverfew have insecticidal properties and can be used in the home to repel moths.

Latin names *Tanacetum parthenium* syn. *Chrysanthemum parthenium, Matricaria parthenium*
Asteraceae
Part used Leaves

🌿 Gardening

Feverfew is a perennial, forming evergreen leafy clumps and producing myriads of small, white-petalled, yellow-centred daisy-like flowers.

Feverfew (*Tanacetum parthenium*)

- **Growing** Feverfew responds well to a sunny position, good soil and good drainage. It self-seeds readily, but you can also grow it from root division. The bitter and highly aromatic leaves act as an insect repellent.
- **Harvesting and storing** Harvest the fresh leaves at any time. (Take note that handling plants can cause dermatitis in some sensitive individuals.)

🌿 Herbal medicine

Tanacetum parthenium. Part used: leaves. Feverfew is used in the treatment and prevention of migraine headaches. If taken over several months, it can lower the frequency of attacks and reduce the severity of symptoms, including visual disturbances and nausea. Fresh leaves of feverfew are sometimes chewed for medicinal purposes; however, commercial preparations are preferable.

Do not use feverfew if you are pregnant or you are breastfeeding.

Migraine medicine

In 1973 in Cardiff, in Wales, Anne Jenkins took three fresh leaves of feverfew a day to cure herself of migraines. After 10 months, as long as she kept taking the leaves, Anne no longer suffered from migraines, which prompted a London migraine specialist to conduct a survey. The clinical trial which followed found that there was a benefit in taking feverfew to prevent migraine.

Flax

Beautiful blue-flowered flax is one of the oldest known crop plants. It produces the fibre used to make linen, flaxseed oil (rich in omega-3) and seeds used in cooking.

Flax (*Linum usitatissimum*)

Latin name *Linum usitatissimum* Linaceae
Parts used Whole plant, seeds, stems

🌿 Gardening

Linum usitatissimum has been cultivated by humans for at least six millennia. The species has been developed as two types: the taller forms known generically as long-stalked flax (for fibre); and the shorter types known as crown flax (for seed production).

Slender, erect, narrow-leafed annuals, in summer, the plants bear single, upward-facing, sky-blue flowers, followed by round capsules, about 1 cm in diameter, filled with glossy, flattened oval seeds. The seed is milled and extracted for flaxseed oil, also known as linseed oil. The industrial-grade oil is used in a range of products, from printing inks to linoleum, while the residual linseed cake is used as cattle feed. The cold-extracted oil is used for human nutritional supplements. Flaxseed is also used in bakery and cereal products.

• **Growing** Flax requires a sunny position and well-drained soil. Sow seed directly into the ground in spring.
• **Harvesting and storing** When mature, cut plants for fibre. Harvest the seed when ripe. Store the seed whole in the refrigerator, or preserve in oil.

🌿 Herbal medicine

Linum usitatissimum. Parts used: seeds, oil. Taken whole or crushed with a little water, the seeds of flax have a gentle laxative effect and are a popular remedy for constipation. The mucilage content of the seed has a soothing effect on inflamed conditions of the gut.

The seed oil is the most concentrated plant source of the omega-3 essential fatty acid, alpha-linolenic acid (ALA), which is often deficient in the Western diet, especially for vegetarians. Human studies indicate that ALA has positive effects on cholesterol levels and a potential role in the treatment of breast, prostate and skin cancers. Taken as capsules or in liquid form, the anti-inflammatory omega-3 oils can also be useful for treating skin conditions such as eczema and psoriasis.

Do not use flaxseed if you are pregnant or you are breastfeeding.

New Zealand flax

Native to New Zealand, *Phormium tenax* (from the family Agavaceae) has been widely adopted for landscaping purposes, as it forms handsome clumps of long, strap-like leaves that have been used in traditional basketry. As a Maori herb, known as harakeke, it is used in a similar way to aloe vera, being applied to wounds and sores, burns and abscesses, ulcers, and rheumatic joints. It has also been used for digestive disorders.

Galangal

There are two types of galangal – greater galangal, which is native to Java, and lesser galangal, originally from the coastal regions of southern China and Vietnam.

Latin name *Alpinia galanga* Zingiberaceae
Also known as Blue ginger, Siamese ginger, Thai ginger
Part used Rhizomes

1. Fingerroot 2. Grated fresh root 3. Whole root 4. Dried ground root 5. Sliced fresh root 6. Sliced dried root 7. Peeled fresh root

Gardening

Widely used in Asian cooking, the white-fleshed rhizomes of greater galangal (*Alpinia galanga*) have a spice and pine fragrance; the flowers, flower buds and cardamom-scented red fruits are all edible. Lesser galangal (*A. officinarum*) has aromatic reddish brown rhizomes that are used medicinally. Fingerroot (*Kaempferia pandurata*), also called Chinese keys, has long, slender finger-like storage roots attached to the rhizome, which is crisp, with a fresh lemony taste.

• **Growing** Galangal requires warm-temperate to subtropical conditions, and rich, moist, well-drained soils. Grow by seed or from rhizome segments; cut them so that each segment contains one or two buds.

• **Harvesting and storing** For fresh culinary use, dig up the rhizomes in late summer or early autumn. Store in a cool, dark place for up to 2 weeks. Dry the root about 10 months after planting. Store dried slices in an airtight container in a dry, dark place for 2 to 3 years.

Herbal medicine

Alpinia officinarum. Part used: rhizomes. In the past, galangal was used traditionally to relieve symptoms of indigestion, including flatulence and nausea. Like ginger, it was reputed to be helpful in alleviating sea-sickness. In North America it was traditionally chewed to calm the stomach and sweeten the breath.

Do not use galangal in greater than culinary quantities if you are pregnant or breastfeeding.

Cooking

Galangal's flavour is similar to ginger's but is not as strong. Greater galangal (*Alpinia galanga*) is the type more often used in cooking, especially in Thailand, but also in Malaysia, Singapore, India and China.

Use the rhizome fresh, or as dried slices (soak in hot water before use), with seafood, in sauces and soups (especially the hot-and-sour ones of Southeast Asia). It features in spicy condiments such as sambals.

If galangal is not available, substitute half the quantity of grated fresh ginger.

Galangal (*Alpinia galanga*)

Seafood coconut soup

100 g flat rice noodles, or noodles of your choice

1 tablespoon peanut oil

3 stalks fresh lemongrass, inner white part finely sliced

5 cm piece galangal, cut into thin slices

1 tablespoon chilli paste

4 cups (1 litre) chicken stock

2 cups (500 ml) coconut milk

2 tablespoons shredded fresh kaffir lime leaves

1 tablespoon palm sugar, finely chopped

1/4 cup (60 ml) fish sauce

400 g firm white fish fillets, cut into 2 cm cubes

8 large green prawns, shelled and deveined, leaving
   tails intact

2 tablespoons lime juice

1 tablespoon roughly chopped coriander leaves, to serve

1 tablespoon roughly chopped fresh Thai basil, to serve

lime wedges, to serve

1 Place noodles in heatproof medium bowl and cover
with boiling water. Stand 10 to 15 minutes, or until
soft. Drain and set aside.

2 Heat oil in large saucepan. Add lemongrass, galangal
and chilli paste; cook, stirring, 1 minute. Add stock
and coconut milk and bring to the boil. Reduce heat
and simmer 5 minutes.

3 Add kaffir lime leaves, palm sugar, fish sauce and
noodles and simmer a further 3 minutes. Add fish;
cook 2 minutes.

4 Add prawns; cook 1 minute, or until prawns turn
pink. Remove from heat. Stir through lime juice,
coriander and basil.

5 Place noodles in serving bowl. Ladle in soup and
serve with lime wedges.

SERVES 6

Garlic & onions

The Sumerians planted onions more than 5000 years ago. The ancient Egyptians valued the pungent bulbs so highly they were often placed in their tombs.

....

Latin name *Allium* sp. Liliaceae
Parts used Leaves, bulbs, bulbils, seed, flowers

Garlic (*Allium sativum*)

Gardening

The alliums — approximately 700 species of them — include not only globe onions, eschallots, leeks, garlic, wild garlic and chives of various kinds, but also exotic forms, such as walking onions and potato onions. Many are so attractive they long ago made their way into the ornamental garden. Alliums are all either bulbous or rhizomatous in habit, characteristically with strap-like or hollow leaves and simple umbels of star-shaped flowers emerging from a papery sheathing bract.

Garlic

Garlic (*A. sativum*) is divided into two groups: 'softnecks' (*A. sativum* var. *sativum*), which contains all the common garlic varieties, and 'hardnecks' (*A. sativum* var. *ophioscorodon*), which contains the remarkable rocambole (serpent garlic or Spanish garlic).

Chives

Four culinary species of chives widely grown for their foliage are: fragrant garlic chives (*A. odorum*) from central Asia, with red-striped white petals; onion chives (*A. schoenoprasum*), with umbels of pink flowers; garlic or Chinese chives (*A. tuberosum*), with white flowers and deliciously garlic-scented, strap-like foliage; and mauve-flowered, garlic-flavoured society garlic (*Tulbaghia violacea*) in both a green and variegated leaf form.

Onions

Common globe onion (*Allium cepa*) is the best known of this aromatic tribe. Spring onions are any variety of onion that is pulled when just beginning to bulb.
Shallots — or eschallots or scallions (*A. cepa*, Aggregatum Group) — form

an above-ground bulb that splits to form a cluster of bulbs with a delicate flavour.

Chinese onion or rakkyo (*A. chinensis*) is an Asian species cultivated for its crisp textured bulbs, which are popularly used raw, pickled or cooked.

Milder-flavoured leeks (*A. porrum*) originate from the Mediterranean. Some excellent varieties include 'Musselburgh', 'Giant Carentan' and 'Bleu Solaise'.

Garlic leek, sweet leek or Levant garlic (*A. ampeloprasum*) is perennial and develops a large basal bulb, which splits into several cloves.

Poor man's leek or Welsh onion (*A. fistulosum*) grows in the same manner as leeks but has hollow leaves. The plant divides at the base, forming a perennial clump.

• **Growing** All the principal *Allium* species require well-tilled and weed-free soil, good drainage and a sunny position. Plant onions by seed. In areas with a short growing season, grow them to the size of bulbils, or sets, in their first season, then plant them out to mature in the second season. Raise chives, cold-tolerant leeks and their relatives by seed. Propagate garlic by planting cloves vertically, with the pointed tip covered by about 2.5 cm of soil.

Regular weeding is essential, particularly in the earlier stages of growth. Do not overwater.

• **Harvesting and storing** If growing species for their aromatic foliage, use them fresh. Harvest globe onions at any stage. When they've stopped growing, the tops of both onions and garlic fall over and wither. Choose a sunny day to pull the bulbs of both types, then leave them for a few days to dry out. Store in a dry, well-ventilated area to prevent fungal rots.

🍃 Herbal medicine

Allium sativum. Part used: bulbs. Research has shown that garlic and several of its constituents have broad-spectrum activity against a variety of disease-causing organisms, including strains of the virus that causes flu. Regular consumption of garlic can help to prevent and

1. Green onions 2. Brown onions 3. Green onions with their tops
4. Red onion 5. Spring onions

treat coughs and colds. To treat infection, you can take up to 2 cloves of garlic a day. Chop and leave for 5 to 10 minutes before cooking. This is to allow the medicinally active component allicin to form. For prevention, aim for a dose of up to 3 cloves a week, or buy a commercial preparation.

Garlic also produces a number of beneficial effects on the cardiovascular system, many of which have been confirmed by clinical trials. Garlic supplementation has been shown to lower cholesterol levels, prevent the hardening of arteries and lessen the risk of blood clot formation. It can also help to reduce blood pressure as well as improve general circulation.

Do not use garlic in greater than culinary quantities if you are pregnant or breastfeeding.

During the First World War, garlic juice was used in field dressings to prevent gangrene.

Chives

Depending on which variety is used, chives (*A. schoenoprasum*) have a mild onion or garlic flavour that goes well with sauces, stews, mashed vegetables such as potatoes, fish, poultry and egg dishes (especially scrambled eggs), and cream cheeses and salad dressings.

The delicate flavour is easily destroyed by heat, so add chives during the last few minutes of cooking time, or scatter them on a finished dish to garnish.

Snip chives with scissors, rather than chop them with a knife. They are essential (along with chervil, parsley and tarragon) in the French herb blend called fines herbes. Snip chives finely and freeze them in ice-cube trays to preserve. The flowers make a pretty garnish.

Chives bear pale purple to pale pink bell-shaped umbels of flowers in summer.

Elephant garlic

Native to the Mediterranean and the Middle East, the giant cloves of elephant garlic (*A. ampeloprasum* 'Elephant') have a sweet flavour that is much less pungent than the garlic commonly used in cooking. The plant is actually a member of the leek family (one of its common names is perennial sweet leek). Eat the cloves raw or cook them like onions.

Cooking

Garlic complements almost any savoury dish, and goes well with most culinary herbs and spices. It is an essential ingredient in many cuisines, especially Asian, Mexican, Mediterranean, Middle Eastern and Caribbean. Even if you don't like the taste of garlic itself, a small amount will enhance the flavour of many dishes.

Garlic comes in white-, pink- and purple-skinned varieties, and in a range of sizes. Choose firm bulbs that are not sprouting, and that are tightly encased in their husks. Peeled cloves should be creamy white, not grey or yellow. Remove any areas of discolouration before using, as these will impart a rank taste to the dish.

When peeled, then sliced or chopped, the enzymes within a clove of garlic react on exposure to air to produce a strong, lingering, sulphurous aroma. The flavour of garlic is similarly strong and sharp, and gives the impression of heat on the palate. The more finely it is crushed or chopped, the stronger garlic's aroma becomes. When cooked properly, the flavour is mellow and sweet. Try baking a whole head in foil, then squeeze out the contents of the cloves. This mellow, creamy paste is delicious spread on bread or cooked meats or stirred through mashed vegetables such as potato.

Take care when cooking garlic; if it is cooked over too high a heat, it will burn, become bitter and taste

Remove any small green shoots from the centre of a cut garlic clove, as these can make food taste bitter.

unpleasant. Even a tiny amount of burnt garlic will permeate and spoil a whole dish.

Garlic is used raw in aïoli (a French garlic mayonnaise) and tapenade (olive paste). Crushed garlic mashed into butter is a delicious and simple sauce for cooked meats, or it can be spread on a sliced loaf or baguette, wrapped in foil and baked in a medium-hot oven for 10 minutes or so. Push slivers of garlic into slits in a joint of lamb or pork, or put a few cloves inside the cavity of a chicken before roasting.

Various processed forms of garlic are commercially available, including crushed pastes and dehydrated flakes, powders and granules. If you are using commercial garlic pastes in a recipe, you may need to make adjustments for the flavour of the salt and vinegar that are often added as preservatives. Garlic is also used in many commercial spice blends, including herb salt, garlic salt and pizza seasoning.

How to peel garlic

Peeling large quantities of garlic is rather tedious. If you're peeling garlic that is to be sliced or chopped, first thump the clove with the flat blade of a large knife. This will distort and crack the skin, making it easier to remove. If you want to use the cloves whole, use a commercially available gadget consisting of a small flexible rubber tube; place the unpeeled cloves in this and roll the tube on a work surface for a few seconds. When you tip out the contents, the cloves should be neatly separated from their husks.

Onion soup

1 tablespoon olive oil
1 tablespoon butter
1.25 kg brown onions, halved and thinly sliced
2 teaspoons soft brown sugar
1 tablespoon plain flour
4 cups (1 litre) chicken or beef stock
1 baguette, cut into 12 slices about 1.5 cm thick
1 cup (130 g) grated gruyère

1 Heat the olive oil and butter in a large deep saucepan. Cook the onions and cook over medium–low heat for 15 minutes, stirring occasionally. Increase heat to medium and cook for another 20 minutes, until golden brown.

2 Stir in sugar and flour, mixing well. Pour in stock and 2 cups (500 ml) water, stirring well. Bring to the boil. Reduce heat and simmer for 15 minutes, until the mixture is slightly thickened.

3 Just before serving, preheat the grill to high. Grill bread on both sides until lightly golden. Sprinkle with cheese, briefly grill until melted.

4 Ladle soup into warm bowls. Top each with three toasts. Serve quickly before bread goes soggy.

SERVES 4 (MAKES ABOUT 7 CUPS/1.75 LITRES)

Ginger

Ginger was highly recommended by none other than Confucius, who is said to have flavoured all his food with it. Its medicinal uses include treating motion sickness.

Latin name *Zingiber officinale* Zingiberaceae
Part used Rhizomes

🍃 Gardening

Native to tropical Asia, ginger is a rhizomatous perennial growing to about 90 cm high, producing many fibrous leaf stalks. The plump rhizomes, known as 'hands', are pale yellow when freshly dug. The spring shoots and flower buds of Japanese or myoga ginger (*Z. mioga*) are popular in Japanese cuisine, and cassumar ginger (*Z. cassumar*) is used in Southeast Asia.

• **Growing** Ginger grows best in rich, moist, well-drained soil and requires warm-temperate to subtropical conditions. Grow by seed or from rhizome segments, cut so that each segment contains one or two buds.

• **Harvesting and storing** For fresh culinary use, dig up the rhizomes in late summer or early autumn. If drying, do so about 10 months after planting.

🍃 Herbal medicine

Zingiber officinale. Part used: rhizomes. Ginger has been clinically proven as a safe remedy for the prevention and treatment of nausea. It can also benefit other digestive disorders such as indigestion and colic.

It is traditionally used to relieve various conditions associated with 'cold' symptoms as well as period pain, cold hands and feet, arthritis and rheumatism. It may also help protect the heart and blood vessels by preventing the formation of blood clots and lowering cholesterol levels.

🍃 Cooking

Young ginger is tender and sweet, with a spicy, tangy, warm to hot flavour. Older ginger is stronger, hotter and more fibrous. Japanese ginger (*Z. mioga*), known as gari, is widely used as a sushi condiment.

In Asian, Caribbean and African cuisine, ginger is an essential ingredient in curries, stews, soups, salads, pickles, chutneys, marinades, stir-fries, and meat, fish and vegetable dishes. Fresh ginger's uses are mostly savoury; crystallised ginger is used in baked goods, or eaten on its own as confectionery, often sugar-coated.

Dried ginger is hotter than fresh ginger. Ground dried ginger is used in baking and in commercial spice mixtures. Both ground dried ginger and ginger essential oil are used in commercial food flavouring, while ginger extracts are used in cordials, ginger beer and ginger ale.

Ginger root
(*Zingiber officinale*)

Storing and preserving

Select clean, plump, firm rhizomes, then wrap them tightly in foil and store in the vegetable crisper of the refrigerator for several weeks. For long-term storage, ginger may be pickled, preserved in sherry or other strong spirit, or crystallised. Store crystallised ginger or ginger in syrup in an airtight container in a cool, dry place. They will keep for up to 1 year.

Baked fish with ginger and spring onions

4 bream, snapper or other firm white fish fillets,
   (150 g each), skin removed

1½ tablespoons salt-reduced soy sauce

3 teaspoons dry sherry

1 tablespoon grated fresh ginger

2 teaspoons sesame oil

2 spring onions, thinly sliced

1 Preheat the oven to 190°C. Line a baking tray with foil, leaving a 5 cm overhang on short ends. Spray foil with cooking spray. Place fish in the dish in a single layer.

2 Combine soy sauce, sherry, ginger and sesame oil in a small bowl; spoon mixture over the fish. Fold the foil over fish to seal loosely. Bake for 8 to 10 minutes until fish is just cooked through.

3 Carefully lift out foil-wrapped fish. Transfer fish fillets to individual serving plates. Spoon pan juices over the fillets, then sprinkle with sliced spring onions.

SERVES 4

Ginkgo

The ginkgo dates back to the time of the dinosaurs, before the evolution of flowering plants. A remarkable survivor, it is now one of our most popular herbal medicines.

....

Latin name *Ginkgo biloba* Ginkgoaceae
Also known as Maidenhair tree
Parts used Fruits, leaves

🌿 Gardening

The sole remaining species of the once abundant plant order Ginkgoales, which dates back 250 million years, ginkgo has long been cultivated in Japan and China as a sacred tree. The species is dioecious, so the unpleasant smelling plum-like fruit are formed only where male and female trees are grown together.

The 'fruits' are naked seeds, as true fruits only developed with the rise of the flowering plants. Within is a seed resembling an almond, prized in both China and Japan, which is boiled, roasted or baked before being cracked open. The tree is deciduous, colouring a clear gold in autumn. Most varieties of ginkgo were selected for ornamental purposes and include 'Jade Butterfly' and the male clone 'Autumn Gold'.

- **Growing** Ginkgo is fully hardy, suited to a cool climate, and prefers a sunny position and well-drained, fertile soil. It is very slow-growing. You can propagate ginkgo by seed, and if you require fruit, plant a male with a female. Grow named varieties by grafting or by cuttings of semi-ripe wood.

- **Harvesting and storing** Harvest ripe fruits when they fall from the tree and extract the almond-like seed. Harvest the leaves and dry them as they begin to change colour in autumn.

Ginkgo (*Ginkgo biloba*)

Fan-shaped leaves make ginkgo an attractive ornamental tree.

🌿 Herbal medicine

Ginkgo biloba. Part used: leaves. Pharmacological actions associated with ginkgo leaf include potent anti-oxidant and anti-inflammatory effects, an ability to enhance blood flow through arteries, veins and capillaries, as well as a protective effect on many cells of the body against toxin damage. Ginkgo has been shown to be beneficial for the treatment of some circulatory disorders, including Raynaud's syndrome, where there is poor circulation to the hands and feet. Because it improves blood flow to the brain, it is also the world's most popular memory tonic, with claims that it can be of benefit in early-stage dementia.

Ginkgo extract is available in the form of tablets and tinctures from most pharmacies and health food stores. It takes a month or two for ginkgo to reach its maximum effect, so use it for 6 to 12 weeks before assessing whether or not it is helping.

For the safe and appropriate use of ginkgo, consult a healthcare professional. Do not use ginkgo if you are pregnant or breastfeeding.

Tree of hope

Ginkgo has a longstanding association with improvement in brain function and mood, especially in older people. Human trials have shown positive effects on memory impairment and poor concentration as well as the treatment and prevention of symptoms of some types of dementia, including Alzheimer's disease.

Ginseng

Ginseng has been used in Chinese medicine for at least 5000 years. Today it is valued in Western medicine for its ability to reduce the body's reaction to trauma and stress.

Ginseng root
(*Panax ginseng*)

Latin names *Panax* sp. and *Eleutherococcus senticosus* Araliaceae
Part used Roots

Gardening

Ginseng trees are cultivated throughout Asia for their roots. Chinese (Asian or Korean) ginseng (*Panax ginseng*) is a long-lived deciduous perennial with branched taproots, from which spring long-stalked, divided leaves. Siberian ginseng (*Eleutherococcus senticosus*), which is part of the same plant family, is a deciduous shrub with thick roots. American ginseng (*Panax quinquefolius*) is close in appearance to Chinese ginseng. All three have similar properties and uses.

• **Growing** Plants require full sun to light shade, and need a moist, rich, well-drained soil. *Panax* species require mild summers and cold winters, deep shade and a slightly acidic soil.

• **Harvesting and storing** Harvest ginseng roots in autumn from plants that are usually 6 years or older. Use them fresh or peeled and dried.

Herbal medicine

Korean ginseng (*Panax ginseng*), American ginseng (*P. quinquefolius*), Siberian ginseng (*Eleutherococcus senticosus*). Part used: roots. Modern research has shown that these herbs improve the body's capacity to cope with stress, so they have become popular remedies for enhancing mental function and improving physical performance, and during times of overwork, fatigue, exhaustion or convalescence.

American ginseng has been successfully trialled as a treatment for reducing the incidence of upper respiratory infections. All three ginsengs have also been shown to have blood glucose-lowering effects, and may be of benefit in the treatment of diabetes. Although the ginsengs appear to be of benefit in a range of chronic illnesses, clinical trials investigating these herbs have produced mixed results, perhaps due to the variations in the quality, dose, preparation and duration of the different ginsengs used.

Ginseng is commercially available as capsules or fluid extract, or you can make a tea from the root. For the safe and appropriate use of ginseng, consult a healthcare professional. Do not use these herbs if you are pregnant or breastfeeding.

Ginseng (*Panax ginseng*)

Gotu kola

The reputed extraordinary longevity of Professor Li Chung Yon, who is said to have lived to 256, is attributed to drinking tea made with this Chinese 'long-life herb'.

Latin name *Centella asiatica* syn. *Hydrocotyle asiatica* Apiaceae
Also known as Arthritis herb, Asiatic pennywort
Parts used Whole plant, leaves

🍃 Gardening

Gotu kola is a small, creeping, subtropical to tropical groundcover that spreads by stolons, in a similar way to strawberries and violets, forming plantlets that root into the ground and eventually form a dense mat.

• **Growing** Gotu kola is easily grown in a large pot or a dedicated garden bed filled with free-draining, sandy soil enriched with compost and kept moist. It can be grown in full sun or light shade. It tends to die back, but will reshoot in spring. It can be propagated by seed, but is most easily grown from rooted sections of stolon with at least one plantlet attached. Water regularly.

Gotu kola (*Centella asiatica*)

• **Harvesting and storing** Harvest the leaves and use them fresh as required. Dry the leaves out of direct sunlight: spread them out in a single layer or dry them under warm fan-forced air, then store them in an airtight container for medicinal use and for tea. You can also juice the leaves and add them sparingly to tonics.

🍃 Herbal medicine

Centella asiatica. Parts used: whole plant, leaves. Eastern herbalists regard gotu kola as a nerve tonic that calms and strengthens nerve and brain cells, helping to improve memory and reduce anxiety. It is also believed to slow senility and improve rheumatic problems. For the safe and appropriate use of gotu kola, consult your healthcare professional. Do not use gotu kola if you are pregnant or breastfeeding.

Heartsease

Although it may not be a love potion to heal broken hearts, as once reputed, this pretty European wildflower has a variety of herbal uses.

Latin name *Viola tricolor* Violaceae
Also known as Herb constancy, herb trinity, Johnny-jump-up, love-in-idleness, love-lies-bleeding, wild pansy
Parts used Flowers (culinary), aerial parts (medicinally)

Gardening

Heartsease is a spreading, low-growing herb, which flowers profusely in spring and summer. The tiny pansy-like flowers usually have a purple spur and upper petals, with the remaining petals coloured purple, white and yellow with 'pussy whisker' markings.

• **Growing** Heartsease prefers a moist, cool location in dappled shade. In these conditions it will readily reseed.
• **Harvesting and storing** For culinary purposes, harvest the fresh flowers at any time. The aerial parts of the plant are harvested for medicinal use, usually when in full flower. To dry the plants, hang them upside-down in a well-ventilated place away from direct sun.

Herbal medicine

Viola tricolor. Parts used: aerial parts. Heartsease is used to treat eczema and other weeping skin conditions, and is administered either as an infusion or topically in the form of a compress.

Cooking

Many herbs, including heartsease, have edible flowers, which look pretty in a salad. Mix a variety of salad greens with heartsease flowers (the green parts removed) and the flowers of nasturtium, borage, bergamot, fennel or calendula. Add a light dressing. The flowers can also be crystallised for cake decoration or frozen in ice cubes for summer drinks.

Heartsease (*Viola tricolor*)

Crystallised flowers

Crystallised flowers are available from shops that sell cake-decorating supplies. Alternatively, it's easy to make your own. Cupcakes provide an ideal platform for your creative skills.

12–24 heartsease, rose, violet, or other edible flowers or petals
1 eggwhite, at room temperature
1 cup (230 g) caster sugar

1 Combine eggwhite in a small dish with a few drops of water. Using a fork, beat lightly until the white just shows bubbles. Place sugar in shallow dish.

2 Hold a flower or petal in one hand; with other hand, dip a small paintbrush into eggwhite and gently paint flower or petal, covering it completely but not excessively.

3 Gently sprinkle sugar over flower or petal. Place on wire rack covered with baking paper to dry. Repeat with remaining flowers or petals.

4 Allow flowers or petals to dry completely before use (about 12 to 36 hours, depending on humidity). Store crystallised flowers or petals in airtight container until required.

Hops

Malted grains used for brewing beer are very sweet and keep very poorly, so many bitter herbs, like hops, have been used to improve its flavour and help preserve it.

∙∙

Latin name *Humulus lupulus* Moraceae
Parts used Strobiles (cones), shoots, flowers, leaves, vines

Gardening

Hops forms a perennial vine that reaches 10 m. Only female plants produce the required small, cone-like inflorescences called strobiles. The leaves resemble those of a grape vine and are used as a brown dye, while the vines are used for paper-making and basketry.

∙ **Growing** Hops is very adaptable but prefers an open, sunny position and a moist, humus-rich soil. Hops can be raised from seed. Only the female plants are required, so propagate either by root division in spring or from cuttings taken in summer.

For the home garden, train hops on a tall tripod or pyramid support. In hop fields, traditionally vines are trained on tall poles. Clean away all dead material in winter.

Hops
(*Humulus lupulus*)

∙ **Harvesting and storing** Young shoots are harvested in spring for culinary use. Strobiles are harvested in autumn and dried. Both the pollen and leaves can cause allergic responses.

Herbal medicine

Humulus lupulus. Part used: female flowers (strobiles). Hops has mild sedative properties and is commonly prescribed with other relaxing herbs for insomnia, particularly when there is difficulty falling asleep.

The heavily scented essential oil is believed to be responsible for the plant's relaxing effects on the nervous system; the dried flowers can be used in pillows, placed by the bed to induce sleep (to make a herbal sleep pillow, see *page 111*). Hops' calming effects can also help in reducing anxiety.

For insomnia, infuse up to 1 g of dried hops in boiling water and drink 1 cup an hour before bedtime. Hops can also be used to make a relaxing decoction for the bath. Hops has a gently stimulating effect on sluggish digestion due to the presence of bitter compounds, and it is a useful remedy for gastrointestinal complaints, particularly when they are exacerbated by tension and stress.

Do not use hops if you are pregnant or if you are breastfeeding.

Hopped beer

Brewed in ancient Egypt, hopped beer was mentioned by the Roman writer Pliny, who relished eating the plant's spring growth when it was prepared like asparagus. Hops became widely used in Europe, but in England other bitter herbs were preferred until the 16th century, in part because there was a belief that hops could cause melancholia. Some herbal authorities still advise that patients suffering from depression should avoid hops.

Horseradish & wasabi

Horseradish has been cultivated in the eastern Mediterranean region for more than 3500 years. Wasabi, native to Japan, has been cultivated since the 10th century.

....

Latin name *Armoracia rusticana* and *Wasabia japonica* syn. *Cochlearia wasabi* Brassicaceae
Parts used Root and leaves (horseradish); rhizomes (wasabi)

Gardening

Horseradish and wasabi both belong to the same botanical family, Brassicaceae.

Horseradish

Horseradish (*Armoracia rusticana*) is a hardy perennial that forms a rosette of long leaves. The 30 or more strains in cultivation include 'Bohemian', 'Swiss' and 'Sass', and almost all of them are sterile. Below ground, horseradish forms a taproot that expands in diameter in the second and third year. The grated root has been used since ancient times as a pungent condiment and in medicinal preparations.

Horseradish (left) and wasabi

Wasabi

Native to Japan, wasabi or Japanese horseradish (*Wasabia japonica*) is a semi-aquatic perennial with long-stemmed, heart-shaped leaves.

Peel and finely grate fresh wasabi root for use as a condiment.

Below ground is a thick, knobbly rhizome which has a very hot taste similar to horseradish.

• **Growing** Horseradish requires a sunny position and a well-dug soil enriched with rotted compost. Grow wasabi in very clean, cool, slightly alkaline running water, with plenty of shade. The temperature should be between 10°C and 13°C.

In spring, plant pencil-thin sections of lateral horseradish roots horizontally, or up to an angle of 30° from the horizontal. Cover with soil, and firm down. Propagate wasabi from offsets of the rhizome. Don't let horseradish dry out, or the roots will become bitter. Keep wasabi well-shaded, cool and watered.

A number of leaf-eating insects can be a problem for horseradish.

Pick horseradish leaves when young and tender to add to mixed leaf salads or to cook as a vegetable.

• **Harvesting and storing** Dig up horseradish roots and use them fresh at any time in the second and third year; they are at their peak in flavour after the first frost. Store clean roots in sealed plastic bags in the refrigerator for up to 2 months.

Herbal medicine

Armoracia rusticana, Wasabia japonica. Part used: roots or rhizomes. The hot and pungent nature of these roots is due to the presence of compounds responsible for many of their medicinal properties.

Horseradish is antimicrobial and acts as a nasal, sinus and bronchial decongestant, making it a popular remedy for colds and respiratory tract infections. Wasabi is believed to have therapeutic effects similar to those of horseradish.

Do not use these herbs in greater than culinary quantities if you are pregnant or breastfeeding.

Cooking

Young horseradish leaves can be eaten as a vegetable, but the root is the part most often used. Peel and grate it as needed, as it loses its pungency soon after grating, or when heated. Alternatively, grate the root (in a well-aired place to avoid the fumes), adding 1/2 cup (125 ml) white wine vinegar and 1/4 teaspoon salt to each cup (250 ml) of pulp. Store, covered, in the refrigerator. Use as a condiment for beef or fresh or smoked fish.

Wasabi, often in paste form, is served with sushi, sashimi, soba noodles and other Japanese dishes.

Rapid decongestant

If you've ever tasted horseradish (or its Japanese cousin wasabi), you'll know of its ability to clear the sinuses and ease breathing almost immediately. This effect is due to the ability of compounds called glucosinolates to liquefy thickened mucus, making it easier to clear and relieving the pressure and head pain associated with sinus congestion. These are the same compounds that give horseradish its spicy taste. They also have antimicrobial properties, so horseradish helps fight sinus infections, too.

The good news is that you can take the treatment as a tasty condiment in the form of horseradish or wasabi paste. Pills and capsules are also available.

Potato and horseradish salad

1 kg small kipfler or baby potatoes, halved
2 small heads of witlof, leaves separated
½ cup (20 g) chopped fresh flat-leaf parsley
2 tablespoons roughly chopped fresh tarragon
½ cup (60 g) roughly chopped walnuts
juice of 1 lemon
1 tablespoon grated fresh horseradish root
200 g crème fraîche or sour cream

1 Cook potatoes in large saucepan of boiling water until tender. Drain; cool briefly.

2 Place potatoes in large bowl. Add witlof leaves, parsley, tarragon and walnuts; toss to combine.

3 Combine lemon juice, horseradish and crème fraîche in a small bowl; season with sea salt. Pour dressing over potatoes; toss to combine.

SERVES 6

Horsetail

The forests where dinosaurs once roamed were full of giant horsetails, some the height of large trees. Today, their few remaining relatives are tiny by comparison.

Latin names *Equisetum arvense, E. hyemale*
Equisetaceae
Also known as Pewterwort, scouring rush
Part used Sterile stems

Gardening

Horsetails have slender, hollow, jointed stems with leaves that are reduced to scales. The plants have a deep root system and can spread by rhizomes. Horsetails are divided botanically into two major groups: the horsetails, which have whorled branches, and the scouring rushes, which are unbranched.

• **Growing** Horsetails are primarily located around water sources. You can grow the plant in moist soil from pieces of rhizome or divisions in spring. Horsetail can be a very invasive weed, both hard to control and resistant to herbicides. Livestock can be poisoned by long-term grazing. In Australia it is a prohibited weed.

Scouring rush

Rich in silica, horsetails were once every cook's blessing. The hardened longitudinal siliceous ridges on the stems were utilised in ancient Roman times through to the 18th century for scrubbing pots and pans. Horsetail stems were found to be particularly effective for cleaning and polishing pewterware, hence one of the plant's common names – pewterwort. The silica also provided a natural type of non-stick coating for cookware.

• **Harvesting and storing** Harvest the stems in mid- to late summer and dry them.

Herbal medicine

Equisetum arvense. Part used: stems. Horsetail has astringent and tissue-healing properties due to its high silica content. Combined with its gentle diuretic action, it is used to treat mild inflammatory and infectious conditions of the urinary tract, bladder and prostate gland. It is also used in the management of bedwetting.

For the safe and appropriate use of horsetail, consult a healthcare professional. Do not use if you are pregnant or breastfeeding.

Concentrations of gold have been found in some horsetails — a good indicator for gold prospectors.

Horsetail (*Equisetum hyemale*)

Hyssop

Known since ancient times, this attractive flowering herb was once attributed with purification properties, and for this reason was even used to treat leprosy.

Latin name *Hyssopus officinalis* Lamiaceae
Also known as Gratiola
Parts used Flowering spikes, leaves

Gardening

Hyssop is a semi-evergreen perennial subshrub with long slender spikes of lipped, rich blue, nectar-filled flowers that attract bees and butterflies to the garden.

• **Growing** Hyssop requires a sunny, well-drained position. Sow seed in spring, or grow it from cuttings taken either in spring or autumn. It makes an excellent hedge and can also be used as a trap plant for cabbage white butterfly and as a companion plant for grapes.

• **Harvesting and storing** Harvest the leaves at any time and use them fresh, or dry them out of sunlight before storing them in airtight containers. In summer, pick the flowers to use fresh, or dry them.

Herbal medicine

Hyssopus officinalis. Parts used: aerial parts. Hyssop is used to alleviate conditions of the respiratory tract and

Hyssop (*Hyssopus officinalis*)

is therefore often prescribed for colds, flu, feverish conditions, bronchitis and coughs. It is also reputed to have a calming effect on the nerves and has been used to help bring on delayed periods, particularly when the cause is due to tension and stress.

For the safe and appropriate use of hyssop, consult your healthcare professional. Do not use hyssop if you are pregnant or breastfeeding.

The bitter mint-tasting leaves are used to flavour rich foods such as game and pâté.

Hyssop (*Hyssopus officinalis*)

Iris

Irises include several herbal species with rhizomes, known as orris root, which have uses ranging from perfumery (as a fixative) to flavouring gin and chewing gum.

Latin name *Iris* sp. Iridaceae
Part used Rhizomes

Gardening

Iris x *germanica* 'Florentina' and the Dalmatian iris (*I. pallida* 'Dalmatica') are used for commercial orris production. 'Florentina' is a tall bearded iris with white, sweetly scented flowers. The beautiful ceremonial white-flowered *I.* x *germanica* 'Albicans' is still planted on Muslim graves in the eastern Mediterranean.

Heraldic emblem

The yellow flag (*I. pseudacorus*) is the *fleur de lis* of heraldry. In the 12th century, the French kings were the first to use an image of the flower on their shields and later, English kings used it to emphasise their claims to the French throne. Its resemblance to a spearhead is seen as an appropriate symbol of martial power and strength.

- **Growing** *Iris pallida* 'Dalmatica' and *I.* x *germanica* 'Florentina' need well-drained soil and full sun. Grow from divisions of rhizomes that have at least one leaf fan attached and plant the rhizomes horizontally so that only the lower half is buried in the soil. Rhizome rots occur in poorly drained or shaded plants.
- **Harvesting and storing** In late summer, dig rhizomes, clean and dry them, and cure for 2 years to intensify the violet fragrance.

Herbal medicine

Iris versicolor. Part used: rhizomes. A relative of garden irises, blue flag, in combination with other cleansing herbs, has long been used to treat to skin problems.

For the safe and appropriate use of blue flag, consult your healthcare professional. Do not use blue flag if you are pregnant or breastfeeding.

Around the home

Orris root, a greyish powder with the aroma of violets, is derived from the root of the Florentine iris. It is used less for its scent than for its fixative ability — that is, it slows the evaporation of essential oils and prolongs the life of pot-pourris. Orris root can be sprinkled around the edges of areas of carpet or under rugs to deter, although not kill, moths and destructive carpet beetles.

Iris (*Iris* sp.)

Pot-pourri

As far back as the 12th century, sweet-scented herbs and flowers were salted and left to ferment or rot into potently perfumed mixtures, which were then used to disguise household odours and, it was believed, help prevent the spread of disease. Today's pot-pourris are somewhat easier to prepare, and more decorative, than their medieval counterparts.

Rose and lavender pot-pourri

1 cup (10 g) dried rosebuds and/or petals

1 cup (30 g) dried lavender flowers

1 cup (10 g) dried rose geranium leaves

peel of 1 orange, cut into thin strips before drying

2 tablespoons whole cloves, lightly crushed

1 tablespoon whole allspice (pimento), lightly crushed

5 cinnamon sticks, broken into pieces

2 tablespoons orris root powder

6 to 10 drops lavender essential oil

1/2 teaspoon rose geranium essential oil

1   Combine all the ingredients, mix well. Put in a sealed container and leave for a few weeks to mature.

2   To use, transfer to open bowls and stir gently to release the scent.

Rosemary pot-pourri

1 1/2 cups (100 g) dried rosemary leaves

1/4 cup (5 g) dried peppermint leaves

1/4 cup (30 g) whole cloves, lightly crushed

1/4 cup (20 g) crumbled cinnamon sticks

1/4 cup (60 g) orris root powder

1/4 teaspoon rosemary essential oil

Mix the ingredients together and use as for Rose and lavender pot-pourri (above).

Jasmine

Jasmine — the delicate floral emblem of Indonesia, Pakistan and the Philippines — is renowned for its superb sensuous scent, and the very valuable essential oil it yields.

....

Latin name *Jasminum* sp. Oleaceae
Also known as Jessamine
Parts used Flowers, roots

Angel wing jasmine (*Jasminum nitidum*)

🍃 Gardening

'Jasmine' comes from the Persian 'yasmin' which means 'gift from God'. Common jasmine (*J. officinale*) is a tall twining climber with intensely fragrant flowers. Brought to Europe in the 16th century, it is now cultivated commercially for its flowers in southern France, Spain, India, Egypt, China, Algeria and Morocco.

Arabian jasmine (*J. sambac*) forms an arching bush and is native to India. It is used to make a fragrant tisane in China, the blossoms being hand-picked early in the morning and mixed with dried green or oolong tea. Double-flowered forms of *J. sambac* favoured for garlands and religious ceremonies include the rose-like 'Duke of Tuscany'. Angel wing jasmine (*J. nitidum*) is another fragrant, white-flowered species.

• **Growing** Plants prefer a well-drained soil enriched with rotted compost and require a warm climate.

• **Harvesting and storing** Gather fully developed buds in the early morning and add the opening flowers to tea. You can dry them for herbal use.

🍃 Natural beauty

The softening and smoothing effects of jasmine essential oil help to improve the skin's elasticity, and make it particularly helpful in preparations for dry, irritated, sensitive or ageing skin. A calming, jasmine-scented bath before bedtime may improve sleep and reduce anxiety.

Common jasmine (*Jasminum officinale*)

Jasmine essential oil

The delicate, star-shaped flowers of this evergreen vine are distilled to form an essential oil with a rich, warm floral scent with musky overtones that is important in perfumery. Jasmine oil blends well with other 'floral'-style oils, such as rose, and with spicy scents such as sandalwood, It is used in massage blends to relieve stress and anxiety and in aromatherapy as an antidepressant and relaxant.

Essential oils are used in aromatherapy and massage to relax the body and lift the spirits.

Lavender

Fragrant lavender has a host of medicinal uses, many applications around the home and the essential oil is used in homemade air-fresheners and cleaning products.

Latin name *Lavandula* sp. Lamiaceae
Part used Flowers

🍃 Gardening

There are about 30 species of lavender. All are woody-based subshrubs with aromatic foliage and bearing spikes of fragrant flowers. Most important for their medicinal uses are true lavender (*L. angustifolia)* and spike lavender (*L. latifolia*).

In Europe lavender is harvested from July to September, when the crop is in full bloom, often using a hand scythe.

True lavender

L. angustifolia syn. *L. vera*, *L. officinalis*, or 'English' lavender, occurs in the wild in southern Europe at altitudes of 500 to 1500 m. It has been grown in France on a large scale for the perfume trade since the 17th century, and the essential oil it yields is highly valued in the perfumery industry, herbal medicine and aromatherapy. The varieties grown for essential oil production include the great 'Maillette', 'Matheronne', 'Fring', 'Heacham Blue', 'No. 9' and 'Norfolk J2'.

Both fresh and dried flowers are used in cooking (including herb mixtures such as herbes de Provence) and craftwork, for which the finest variety is 'Super-Blue'. Make sure that any flowers you use for culinary purposes have not been sprayed with garden chemicals.

To deter bugs, crumble dried leaves into boxes of documents or drop crushed leaves behind shelved books.

Lavandula sp.

Spike lavender

Sometimes called *Nardus italica*, spike lavender (*L. latifolia* syn. *L. spica*) is endemic to Spain, France, Italy and the Balkan Peninsula, and grows in the wild at much lower altitudes than *L. angustifolia*. The plant has a lavender and camphor scent, and is the source of oil of aspic (*oleum spicae*).

Intermedia lavenders

In the overlap zone on mountainsides where both *L. angustifolia* and *L. latifolia* grow, hybridisation occurs, resulting in plants with intermediate characteristics. They are larger and stronger-growing than true lavender, more tolerant of humidity and yield twice the volume of essential oil compared with true lavender. The oil contains perceptible camphor and is valued at approximately half that of true lavender. It is widely used for personal and household toiletries.

Woolly lavender

L. lanata has leaves that are heavily felted with hairs, and long spikes of scented flowers. It is best grown in large pots in full sun.

Stoechas lavenders

These lavenders have compressed flower spikes shaped rather like a pineapple surmounted by flag-like sterile bracts. All of them are suited to low-altitude warm-climate gardens, including those near the sea.

• **Growing** All lavenders require excellent drainage and full sun. They are better grown fairly hard, and a slow-release fertiliser or a light application of organic compost is recommended. They are all suited to being grown in large pots. Varieties are propagated by cuttings, but species are seed-sown in spring. Prune annually, preferably in early spring. True and intermedia lavenders can be shaped during harvesting. Never cut back hard into old wood, or the plants may die.

• **Harvesting and storing** Harvest true and intermedia lavenders in midsummer when spikes are one- to two-thirds open. Tie lavender stems in bunches and hang them upside-down to dry. Strip them of their flowers or dry on screens in an airy place.

Cotton lavender

Also known as santolina, cotton lavender (*Santolina chamaecyparissus*) has a compact habit that makes it ideal for a low hedge or edging a path. Its grey, toothed aromatic leaves have a similar scent to lavender and are very useful for repelling moths. Add the dried leaves to moth-repellent sachets and place dried bunches with stored blankets and other woollens. Silverfish also hate santolina.

L. dentata, one of the stoechas lavenders

Herbal medicine

Lavandula angustifolia. Part used: flowers.
An age-old remedy for calming and soothing the nerves, improving mood and relaxing muscles, beautifully scented lavender and its essential oil are commonly used for inducing a restful sleep, relieving depression and anxiety and for other disorders relating to a nervous or tense state, including stomach upsets.

Lavender flowers can be taken as an infusion or added to a bath to soothe and aid in relaxation. Lavender essential oil can be used to treat blemished skin, and applied to relieve the sting of insect bites or to prevent cuts and grazes becoming infected. You can add essential oil to massage oil to help relieve muscle tension and headaches.

For the safe and appropriate internal use of lavender, consult your healthcare professional. Do not use lavender if you are pregnant or breastfeeding.

Around the home

If you could only choose one herb for household use, lavender would have to be at the top of the list. Apart from its pretty flower and much-loved scent, lavender is antibacterial, antibiotic, antiviral, antiseptic, deodorising and insect repelling, which means that you can use it in the living room, kitchen, bathroom, laundry, nursery and patio, as well as in your wardrobes and drawers, on your pets and on your skin.

- Use both the dried flowers and leaves to make moth-repellent sachets and lavender bags — they both contain the aromatic oil that insects hate.
- Infuse distilled white vinegar with the flowers and leaves, fresh or dried, for an inexpensive and very effective spray for cleaning and disinfecting a variety of surfaces.
- Add a few drops of lavender essential oil to environmentally friendly unscented kitchen and laundry cleaning products for a fresh, natural scent.

Lavender linen water

Known in France as *eau de linge*, this spray imparts a beautiful fresh lavender scent when used to dampen clothes and linen before ironing. It can also be used to spritz still-damp washing before hanging it out to dry.

¼ teaspoon lavender essential oil
40 ml vodka
2 cups (500 ml) demineralised
   water (from the laundry section
   of supermarkets)

Combine the lavender essential oil and vodka in a clean, dry glass bottle. Replace the lid and leave for 24 hours.

Add the water, shake to combine and cap tightly. Transfer to a spray bottle when ironing and use as required.

- Dampen a cotton-wool ball and add a few drops of lavender essential oil. Drop it into your kitchen bin, or the dust container of the vacuum cleaner, to eliminate stale odours.
- For fragrant clothes drying, put several drops of lavender essential oil — or a combination of oils such as lavender, rosemary, lemon and pine — on a damp face washer and throw it into the tumble dryer with a load of damp clothes.

Cooking

Dried lavender flowers are used in the Moroccan spice blend ras el hanout, in the French herbes de Provence and to flavour vinegar and salad dressings. The chopped leaves and flowers, fresh or dried, can be used in marinades and rubs for pork and lamb. Lavender goes well in sweet dishes containing cream, such as ice cream and custards. It can be added to shortbread and icings and used in jams and jellies. Crystallise fresh flowers as edible cake decorations (see *page 89*).

A history of epic proportions

Reputed to have been brought from the Garden of Eden by Adam and Eve, lavender has a history that is almost as old as humankind itself. The ancient Egyptians dipped shrouds in lavender water, while the Romans scented their public baths with it — hence its name, from the Latin word *lavare*, meaning 'to wash'. Under its biblical name 'spikenard', it was popularly supposed to have been used by the Virgin Mary to perfume Jesus's swaddling clothes, by Mary Magdalene to anoint Jesus's feet, and was also favoured in the Middle Ages by apothecary monks, who used it to treat everything from labour pains to demonic possession.

Compresses

A compress is a cloth that has been soaked in an infusion (or a diluted tincture) and applied to the skin. Compresses are used to relieve headaches and pain, disinfect wounds and soothe tired eyes. Make a fresh one each time.

Make a strong infusion of dried herb (lavender flowers are used here), using 2 to 3 teaspoons of dried herb per 1 cup (250 ml) water. Cover the infusion and steep for 10 to 15 minutes. Remove the cover and leave the infusion to cool to a temperature that is comfortable to the skin. Soak a face washer or flannel in the infusion and wring out the excess water.

Usage Apply to the affected part. As the compress dries out, it can be resoaked and reapplied.

Lemon balm

Lemon balm is used in herbal teas, wines and liqueurs and many eau de colognes. Handfuls of the leaves, which contain a lemon-scented oil, were once used to polish wooden furniture.

Latin name *Melissa officinalis* Lamiaceae
Also known as Bee balm, common balm, melissa, sweet balm
Part used Leaves

Gardening

Lemon balm bears a resemblance to its close relations, the mints. The insignificant flowers are lemon-yellow, and borne in clusters on the upper parts of the stems. While the common form of balm has a fresh lemon fragrance, there are varieties with related but different scents, including 'Lime', with a true lime fragrance, and 'Citronella', which mimics the scent of citronella oil and is said to act as an insect repellent.

• **Growing** Lemon balm is an unfussy plant, but prefers full sun to partial shade and a well-drained but moist soil. It also grows well in pots. Lemon balm is a perennial usually grown from seed, although it is easy to raise from cuttings taken in spring and autumn, or from rooted divisions.

• **Harvesting and storing** Harvest the fresh foliage as required. To dry, cut the plant down to about 7.5 cm in mid- to late afternoon, secure the stems in small bunches with rubber bands, and hang upside-down in a well-ventilated area out of direct sunlight. Strip off the dried leaves and store them in airtight containers in a cool place.

Lemon balm (*Melissa officinalis*)

From nymph to bee

Lemon balm's association with bees goes back to ancient times. According to Greek mythology, Melissa was one of the nymphs who hid Zeus from his father Cronus, feeding him milk and honey. Once Zeus ruled Olympus, he changed her into a queen bee.

Lemon balm was once planted around hives to help guide bees back: 'when they are strayed away, they do find their way home by it', observed Pliny, a Roman writer on natural history.

Herbal medicine

Melissa officinalis. Part used: leaves. Lemon balm's mild sedative and mood-enhancing effects are commonly used to treat sleep disorders, restlessness, anxiety and depression. Take as a tea by infusing 1 to 2 teaspoons of fresh leaves in boiling water; drink 1 cup 2 to 3 times a day. Don't use lemon balm if you're pregnant or breastfeeding, except under professional supervision.

Cooking

Lemon balm's lemon scent and lemon-and-mint flavour go with most foods complemented by either of those flavours. Use the leaves in tea, salads, cordials, fruit dishes, wine cups and chilled summer drinks or in stuffings for poultry or fish.

Stagger the heights of complementary pots and containers and underplant tall herbs with trailing plants that will spill over the edge of the pot.

Cleaning with herbs

The beauty of homemade herbal cleaning products is that they're mostly composed of just one main substance — the cleaning agent — which means that you're not paying for bulking additives, artificial colours or perfumes. You can also choose the type and strength of the scent you want; fresh herbs or essential oils almost invariably leave a delightfully fresh, clean smell. So, whether you're already committed to a greener way of cleaning or you just want to save money and simplify your life a little, herbal cleaning makes a lot of sense.

All-purpose herb vinegar spray

This all-purpose, environmentally friendly, non-toxic spray is great to have on hand for wiping, cleaning and deodorising almost every surface (except marble). If you don't have any fresh herbs, add drops of essential oil instead.

fresh or dried herbs (you can also use herbal tea bags)
distilled white vinegar

1 Roughly chop 1 to 2 large handfuls of fresh or dried herbs (such as lemon verbena, peppermint, rosemary, lemon balm or lavender), or place 5 to 10 tea bags in the bottom of a wide-mouthed glass jar.

2 Add vinegar to fill the jar. Replace the lid, leave for a few days to infuse, then strain out the herbs. (If you are using tea bags, you can gently warm the vinegar before pouring to ensure maximum diffusion.)

3 Decant into a plastic spray bottle. This spray is perfectly safe and very effective to use at full-strength, but it can also be diluted half-and-half with water for lighter jobs.

How to use herb vinegar spray

☐ **Keep** your dishwasher clean and fresh: Add ½ cup (125 ml) herb vinegar to the rinse cycle.

☐ **Cut** grease and make glasses sparkle: Add 3 tablespoons herb vinegar to the sink with the dishwashing detergent.

☐ **Dissolve** mineral build-up on clogged shower heads: Soak overnight in diluted herb vinegar.

☐ **Clean** soap scum from a glass shower screen: Mix 2 parts salt with 1 part herb vinegar. Rub onto the screen with a cloth or fine steel wool. Rinse and dry.

☐ **Stop** mould: Mix 2 teaspoons borax and 1 cup (250 ml) herb vinegar. Apply with a cloth, leave for 30 minutes then wipe off.

☐ **Clean** the refrigerator: Wipe out the fridge with herb vinegar, then rub over with a sponge dipped in vanilla essence.

☐ **Remove** mould from refrigerator door seals: Scrub the mould from the folds with an old toothbrush dipped in herb vinegar.

All-purpose non-vinegar herbal cleanser

If you don't want to use vinegar in your herbal cleanser – perhaps because you have marble benchtops that the acid in vinegar can damage – you can still make an all-purpose spray with water and a little extra cleaning power from borax.

fresh or dried herbs (or herbal tea bags)
2 tablespoons borax
herbal essential oil (optional)

1 Prepare the herbs as for the All-purpose herb vinegar spray (opposite).

2 Pour over hot water to cover and allow to steep for a few days. Strain, then add the borax and a few drops of essential oil, if using.

3 Shake to mix well and decant into spray bottles.

Lemon–grapefruit dishwashing liquid

When washing dishes use a tablespoonful of this dishwashing liquid in hot water. You could also use lavender or rosemary essential oil: both are good at cutting grease. As this is a soap, it does not produce as many suds as detergent, but it is still very effective.

3 tablespoons liquid Castile soap
2 cups (500 ml) warm water
2 teaspoons vegetable glycerine
2 tablespoons distilled white vinegar
10 drops lemon essential oil
10 drops grapefruit essential oil

1 Mix all ingredients in a jar, cover and shake well to blend. Store in a plastic squeeze bottle.

Rosemary handwash

This foamy gel is ideal for keeping your hands clean while cooking, and the rosemary essential oil is antibacterial.

¼ to ½ cup (50 to 100 g) pure soap flakes
2 cups (500 ml) very hot water
¼ cup (60 ml) glycerine
½ teaspoon rosemary essential oil (or the herbal essential oil of your choice)

1 Put the soap flakes and the water in a bowl and whisk vigorously until the flakes have dissolved and you have a foam that is rather like whipped egg white. Cool to lukewarm.

2 Stir in the glycerine and the essential oil, whisk again and leave to cool. As the mixture cools, it becomes more solid, but if you have whisked enough, it should remain foamy. If it is too thick for a pump bottle, beat in more water.

3 To use, squirt a little into the palms of your hands, lather and rinse off.

Many herbs are antibacterial, making them natural disinfectants.

Lemongrass

Lemongrass, a tall and attractive tropical grass with a powerful lemon fragrance, is widely used in the cooking of Thailand, Vietnam and other Southeast Asian countries.

∙∙

Latin name *Cymbopogon citratus* Poaceae
Part used Stems

Lemongrass (*Cymbopogon citratus*)

🍃 Gardening

A number of the 56 *Cymbopogon* species are fragrant, but the herb most commonly called lemongrass is West Indian lemongrass (*C. citratus*), one of several species that share this scent. Its narrow, leafy stalks grow in large clumps that reach 1 m or more. East Indian lemongrass or Cochin lemongrass (*C. flexuosus*) is also widely grown for its essential oil. Ceylon citronella (*C. nardus*) and Java citronella (*C. winterianus*) share the lemon-related scent of citronella.

• **Growing** This herb is best suited to a sunny position, well-drained soil and warm growing conditions.
• **Harvesting and storing** Harvest stems as required. Cut the upper green part into segments and dry it out of direct sunlight, then store it in airtight containers and use it for tea. For cooking, wrap the white bulbous lower portion in plastic wrap and store in the refrigerator for several weeks.

🍃 Herbal medicine

Cymbopogon citratus. Part used: stems. Lemongrass tea was traditionally used to treat digestive upsets and to alleviate stomach ache and cramping.

For the safe and appropriate medicinal use of this herb, consult your healthcare professional. Do not use lemongrass in greater than culinary quantities if you are pregnant or breastfeeding.

🍃 Cooking

The strong citrus flavour of lemongrass goes well in Southeast Asian cooking and is often teamed with chillies and coconut milk. Lemongrass is also an excellent addition to Western cooking, particularly in fish and seafood dishes. Use the lower white part of the fresh stems and slice finely crosswise to avoid a fibrous texture in the finished dish. If using a whole stem or large pieces, bruise first to release the flavour and remove before serving.

Natural protection

A natural insect repellent, lemongrass offers some protection from fleas, ticks, lice and mosquitoes. The essential oil can be used in an oil burner. Alternatively, combine a few drops with equal amounts of eucalyptus oil in a water spray bottle and lightly spritz over outdoor furniture on summer evenings. Or, light a candle made with citronella, a close relative of lemongrass.

Chicken lemongrass skewers

600 g chicken mince

1 tablespoon grated fresh ginger

1 cup (30 g) chopped fresh coriander leaves

1 long red chilli, seeded and chopped (optional)

1 clove garlic, crushed

2 tablespoons salt-reduced soy sauce

1 tablespoon lime juice

4 lemongrass stems

canola oil spray, for cooking

lime wedges, to serve

Soy ginger dipping sauce

1/2 cup (125 ml) salt-reduced soy sauce

1 long red chilli, seeded and finely chopped

3 tablespoons grated fresh ginger

2 tablespoons rice vinegar

1 Combine chicken, ginger, coriander, chilli, garlic, soy sauce and lime juice in a bowl. Mix well, using your hands.

2 Place dipping sauce ingredients in a small bowl; stir well to combine. Trim ends of lemongrass stems; cut each in half lengthwise to make 8 skewers.

3 Divide chicken mixture into 8 even portions. Shape one portion around middle of each lemongrass skewer, moulding it with your hands. (This can be done ahead; cover and refrigerate until ready to cook.)

4 Preheat chargrill pan or barbecue hotplate over medium–high heat and lightly spray with a little oil. Cook the skewers for 6–8 minutes, turning occasionally, until golden and cooked through. Serve with dipping sauce and lime wedges.

MAKES 8

Lemon verbena

The fresh, intensely lemon fragrance of this herb, which is native to Peru and Argentina, has long been prized for use in tisanes, liqueurs, cooking, pot-pourri and perfumery.

···

Latin name *Aloysia citriodora* syn. *Lippia citriodora*, syn. *A. triphylla* Verbenaceae
Also known as Herb Louisa, lemon beebrush
Parts used Leaves, flowers

Lemon verbena
(*Aloysia citriodora*)

Gardening

Lemon verbena is a straggly shrub with arching branches and pointed, strongly aromatic leaves. In summer the bush produces tiny, four-petalled, white or pale mauve flowers.

• **Growing** Lemon verbena requires full sun and free-draining rich soil. Propagate by semi-ripe tip cuttings. The plant is cut back by frost, so should be winter mulched in cool climates. In heavy frost areas grow it in a pot and bring it under protection during winter. Trim to shape. Bushes often leaf out very late in spring; don't discard them prematurely.

• **Harvesting and storing** Leaves can be harvested at any time to use fresh. For drying, pick leaves and buds before they flower. It freezes well.

Herbal medicine

Aloysia citriodora syn. *Lippia citriodora* syn. *A. triphylla*. Parts used: aerial parts. Lemon verbena is used as a digestive aid for symptoms of flatulence and colic. It is thought to help with insomnia and nervous agitation. Lemon verbena is also prescribed for feverish conditions.

For the safe and appropriate use of these herbs, consult your healthcare professional. Do not use these herbs if you are pregnant or breastfeeding.

Sweet relation

The herb world offers some extraordinary sweeter-than-sugar plants, one of which is, like lemon verbena, a member of the Verbenaceae family. Aztec sweet herb (*Phyla scaberrima* syn. *Lippia dulcis*) is a frost-tender, semi-prostrate perennial with short, compressed spikes of white flowers and oval leaves that suffuse red in the sun. It contains hernandulcin, which is more than 1000 times sweeter than sugar. Strains high in camphor should be avoided, although the Cuban chemotype has only a trace of camphor.

Paraguay sweet herb (*Stevia rebaudiana*) is a tall perennial in the Asteraceae family. It was the *yerbe dulce* of the Guarani Indians, who used it to sweeten yerba maté, a traditional tea made from a species of holly (*Ilex paraguariensis*). *Stevia* contains stevioside, which is up to 300 times sweeter than sugar.

Cooking

The leaves are best used fresh and young. Use sparingly, otherwise the flavour can overwhelm the food and be reminiscent of lemon-scented soap.

Lemon verbena is a common ingredient in many herbal teas, imparting a wonderfully fragrant flavour. Its lemony taste complements poultry (add it to stuffings) and fish, it can be sprinkled through salads, used to flavour salad dressings and substituted for lemongrass.

The leaves are used to give a lemon flavour to fruit salads and other fruit dishes, desserts and drinks. Infuse them in custard-based sauces for desserts, or finely chop and add to Asian dishes.

Add whole leaves to apple jelly, and chopped young leaves to fruit salads. With its digestive and relaxant properties, the tea is ideal for drinking after dinner.

Around the home

Lemon verbena makes an ideal filling for a herbal sleep pillow (see right). Or you can use it with other lemony leaves, such as lemon-scented geranium, lemon thyme, and lemon balm to make a room-freshening, citrus-scented pot-pourri. Place the mixture in a bowl or push it into sachets to slide down the sides and backs of lounge cushions or inside cushion covers.

Herbal sleep pillow

Rest your head on a pillow filled with aromatic herbs and you'll quickly find yourself relaxing and drifting into an untroubled sleep.

Make your pillow cover from cotton print and the inner pillow from calico or other fine material. You can use one print for the front and the flap of the cover, and a contrasting print for the back. Add ric-rac or bobble braid to decorate.

Fill the inner pillow with a single herb or with a combination of herbs. Take care to choose ones that will help to ease your mental and physical fatigue and also complement each other.

Herbs known for their calming properties include lavender, rose, lemon verbena, chamomile and myrtle. Avoid herbs such as eucalyptus and cinnamon, as their more insistent aromas tend to energise rather than relax.

Make your inner pillow the same size as the cover, leaving an opening for filling. Use a greaseproof paper cone to loosely fill it with the herbs of your choice. Stitch the opening closed, then insert the inner pillow into the cover, using the flap to hold it in place.

Freezing herbs

Freezing herbs is a great way to retain colour and flavour. It is particularly suitable for culinary herbs with very fine leaves or a very high moisture content, and for those that lose their taste when dried.

....

Good candidates for freezing include fennel and dill tips, tarragon, chives, parsley, chervil and basil.

For herbs you intend to use in small quantities or add to wet dishes, such as soups, casseroles and risotto, freezing herbs into ice cubes works perfectly. Rinse fresh herbs under cold running water before chopping them finely. Place a tablespoonful of the chopped herb into each segment of an ice-cube tray, add a little water, and then place the tray in the freezer. When the cubes are frozen, transfer them into a labelled plastic bag or container, and they'll keep for months.

Freeze whole bunches of herbs to use in larger quantities or in recipes that won't benefit from the extra water of the melted ice. After rinsing the herbs, pat them dry with a paper towel and tie them loosely together. Place the whole bunch inside a sealed and labelled plastic bag and store it in the freezer. The frozen herbs will become quite brittle, so before you use them, just scrunch the bag with your hand to break the leaves into pieces.

Another way to store summer herbs for winter use is to chop and freeze a large quantity in a small plastic container.

An ice-cube tray is ideal for freezing small quantities of herbs you tend to use sparingly or add to soups or casseroles.

Freeze whole mint leaves or borage flowers in ice cubes and use them in fruit juices and cocktails.

Licorice

In 1305, Edward I of England taxed imports of licorice to fund repairs to London Bridge. Dominican monks began cultivating licorice in Pontefract, Yorkshire, in the 1500s.

Licorice root

Latin name *Glycyrrhiza glabra* Papilionaceae
Parts used Taproot, rhizomes

Gardening

Licorice is a graceful, arching, deciduous perennial growing to about 1.5 m with long, oval leaves and loose spikes of pale purple flowers. It has a thick, deep taproot and spreads underground via extensive stolons. It grows particularly well on the rich alluvial plains of Turkey which, together with Spain and Greece, is still a leading world supplier.

• **Growing** Licorice prefers a rich soil and a sunny position. New crops are propagated by rhizome segments planted in spring, and by seed.

• **Harvesting and storing** Both the taproot and the rhizomes can be used. They are usually dug when 3 years old and air-dried before being ground and then processed.

Herbal medicine

Glycyrrhiza glabra. Part used: roots. Licorice root's soothing effects and ability to expel mucus make it a common ingredient in many remedies used to treat coughs, bronchitis and catarrhal lung conditions.

A compound called glycyrrhizin, which gives the herb its anise flavour, is responsible for the healing effects of licorice on gastrointestinal ulcers and inflammatory conditions of the digestive system. It also acts as a tonic for the adrenal glands, so licorice is often prescribed as a supportive remedy in times of stress and exhaustion.

For the safe and appropriate use of licorice, consult a healthcare professional. Do not use licorice if you are pregnant or breastfeeding.

Natural beauty

This herb is considered an effective natural lightener for brown age spots. For the best result, pair it with a natural fruit peel containing vitamin C and alpha hydroxy acids to slough off dead skin.

Cooking

Licorice root is one of many spices and herbs used in Chinese master stocks, adding to their intensity and depth of flavour. Add the chopped root sparingly (it can be bitter) when stewing fruit.

Fit for an emperor

Pontefract, or pomfret, cakes became a popular sweet in England in the 16th century. These soft, flat discs made with licorice, gum arabic and sugar were stamped with a stylised image of Pontefract Castle. They are still made and loved, along with another English favourite, the distinctive multicoloured licorice allsorts. It is said that Napoléon Bonaparte always carried licorice lozenges, which were based on pontefract cakes.

Lime

Lime (*Tilia cordata*)

In medieval times the lime (or linden) tree was associated with the Virgin Mary. It was planted for its fragrant healing flowers and to provide shade in monastery gardens.

Latin name *Tilia cordata* syn. *T. parvifolia*, *T.* x *europaea* Tiliaceae
Also known as Linden, tilia
Part used Flowers

Gardening

Called the 'tree of life' due to its many medicinal uses, lime (*T. cordata*) is a deciduous tree (to 10 m) with glossy, dark green, heart-shaped leaves. It is known as the linden tree in Germany and *tilleul* in France. In midsummer, it bears clusters of pale yellow flowers, heavy with fragrance, which attract bees to their copious nectar. Hives placed around flowering trees yield a prized fragrant honey.

Tilia is occasionally confused with the citrus fruit species known as lime (*Citrus aurantifolia*).

Celebrating lime blossom

Linden trees are popular ornamentals in Europe, where the flowering tips are harvested at their peak and air-dried for use in lime blossom tea, a particularly popular tisane in France. The centre of production is Buis les Baronnies, a medieval town that each July celebrates an annual lime blossom festival, together with their annual harvest sales.

- **Growing** *Tilia* prefers a sunny open position. *Tilia* species tend to sucker. Either remove these, or pot them and, when established, plant elsewhere.
- **Harvesting and storing** The petals drop rapidly to allow the fruits to swell so, over a short time interval, harvest flower clusters together with a few attendant young leaves at the peak of flowering. Spread out the flowers and thoroughly air-dry them before storing.

Herbal medicine

Tilia cordata, T. platyphyllos. Parts used: flowers, bracts. Lime flowers are a common ingredient of many herbal teas that are prescribed to help induce a restful sleep, especially in children. The plant has a sedative and calming effect on the nerves and muscles, and can help to reduce restlessness, tension and anxiety.

Lime flowers are a traditional European medicine for high blood pressure, especially when it is caused or worsened by worry. The flowers can also be helpful in the treatment and prevention of atherosclerosis (hardening of the arteries).

Lime flowers are beneficial in feverish conditions such as colds, influenza and other respiratory infections.

To use, infuse 1 teaspoon of dried lime flowers in boiling water and drink up to 3 cups per day.

For the safe and appropriate use of lime flowers, consult your healthcare professional. Do not use lime flowers if you are pregnant or breastfeeding.

Mix colours, shapes and textures from your herb garden to create a unique table centrepiece.

Lovage

Lovage has an intense celery flavour that's perfect for winter dishes. Traditionally used in love potions, it provides generous harvests and has a range of medicinal uses.

Latin name *Levisticum officinale* Apiaceae
Also known as Bladder seed, Cornish lovage, garden lovage, Italian lovage, love parsley
Parts used Leaves, seeds, roots

Gardening

Lovage is native to the eastern Mediterranean and is the only species in its genus, although it is closely related to both angelica and celery. A hardy perennial plant, it has large, frond-like, glossy leaves; the tiny yellow flowers, borne in clusters, are followed by oval seeds (fruits), which can be used like celery seeds in cooking.

Lovage (*Levisticum officinale*)

Love ache

As its common name indicates, lovage, or love ache as it was once called, was traditionally used as an aphrodisiac and an ingredient in love potions and charms. On a more practical note, however, medieval travellers once lined their boots with lovage leaves to absorb foot odours, while a decoction of lovage root and foliage makes an effective body deodorant. Perhaps lovage was less a love potion than a deodorant, making close physical contact more appealing in a period when people rarely washed.

• **Growing** Lovage requires a rich, well-drained soil and light shade where summers are hot. Grow from seed or by division in spring. Cut back older plants to encourage fresh foliage in summer. In a mixed garden, mark the position of lovage, as it is fully deciduous.
• **Harvesting and storing** For cooking, pick the leaves as required. You can dry all parts of the plant and also freeze the leaves in sealed plastic bags.

Cooking

Called *céleri bâtard*, or false celery, by the French, lovage is used as an ingredient in many commercial bouillons, sauces, stocks and condiments; its seeds are added to liqueurs and cordials as well as to breads and sweet pastries. Blanch the stems in the same manner as rhubarb, or eat them raw in salads. You can also candy the stems and eat them as a sweet, or use the leaves in cooking to provide an intense, celery-like flavouring.

Lovage and fennel omelettes

8 large eggs

1/3 cup (80 ml) milk

1 teaspoon salt

1/2 cup (25 g) roughly chopped fresh chives,
  sliced into 2 cm lengths

3 tablespoons roughly chopped fresh lovage

2 tablespoons roughly chopped fresh
  fennel leaves

1 tablespoon butter

1/2 cup (60 g) grated full-flavoured cheese
  such as gruyère

1 Whisk eggs and milk in a large bowl. Season with
   the salt and stir in herbs.

2 Melt butter in small non-stick frying pan over high
   heat. Pour one-quarter of egg mixture into pan. Cook
   about 1 minute, stirring gently, the egg will begin to
   set around edge of pan almost immediately. Using
   a fork or wooden spoon, gently pull back cooked
   egg from edge of pan, allowing any uncooked egg
   mixture to run underneath.

3 Cook a further 45 seconds to 1 minute, or until egg
   is just set. Sprinkle cheese over. Fold over one half of
   omelette and slide onto serving plate. Cover with foil
   to keep warm.

4 Continue with remaining mixture. Serve at once, with
   a crisp mixed salad.

SERVES 4

Mallow & hollyhock

Hollyhock reportedly reached Europe from China via the Holy Land, hence its original name of holy mallow or holyoke. Marsh mallow is widely used medicinally.

Latin name *Althaea officinalis*, *Malva* sp. and *Alcea* sp. Malvaceae
Also known as Cheeses (hollyhock)
Parts used Roots, leaves, flowers, seeds

🌿 Gardening

Mallow and hollyhock contain similar mucilaginous compounds which have soothing effects on inflamed conditions of the respiratory tract.

Marsh mallow (*Althaea officinalis*)

Mallow

Marsh mallow (*Althaea officinalis*) is a tall (up to 1.2 m) perennial with finely hairy, grey-green, coarsely toothed leaves and five-petalled pink flowers.

Musk mallow (*Malva moschata*) is a European perennial with kidney-shaped basal leaves and contrasting, much divided leaves on the upper stems. The leaves and profuse pink (white in the variety 'Alba') flowers are musk-scented.

Hollyhock

The tall flowering stems of hollyhock (*Alcea rosea*) can reach 3 m, and bear single or double flowers — in shades of lemon, apricot, white, pink, red or purple. Leaves are large and rough-textured. All mallows have disc-shaped, nutty-flavoured seeds.

• **Growing** All species prefer a well-drained, moist soil and a sunny position. Grow from seed sown in spring. Stake both hollyhocks and musk mallow in summer. Cut plants down in late autumn.

• **Harvesting and storing** Gather flowers and leaves as required to use fresh or dried. Dig up and dry marsh mallow roots when they are 2 years old.

🌿 Herbal medicine

Althaea officinalis. Parts used: leaves, roots. The plant's botanical name, *Althaea,* comes from the Greek *altha*, meaning 'to cure'. Rich in mucilaginous compounds, the leaves and roots of the marsh mallow have long been used to treat conditions of the respiratory tract, including irritating cough, bronchitis and sore throat. With a higher amount of mucilage, the root is regarded as the more effective.

Marsh mallow root is also used as a topical agent in mouthwashes to treat inflammation of the mouth and throat and as an ointment to soothe eczematous skin conditions.

To use, infuse 2 to 5 g of dried marsh mallow root in cold (not hot) water and seep for 8 hours to release mucilage. Drink up to 3 cups per day.

Malva sylvestris. Parts used: leaf, flower. Due to its similar mucilaginous compounds, mallow has been used for much the same purposes to marsh mallow, although it is considered less potent. Like marsh

Hollyhock (*Alcea rosea*)

mallow, it is used for respiratory and gastrointestinal conditions, characterised by inflammation and irritation, that benefit from the plant's soothing properties.

Do not use these herbs if you are pregnant or you are breastfeeding.

Cooking

Both the young leaves and the flowers of mallow and hollyhock are edible, and can be added to salads. Young leaves can also be cooked, like spinach. A herbal tea can be made from hollyhock petals.

Marshmallow

Confectionery marshmallow was once made from the mucilage in the roots of marsh mallow. The use of sweetened pastilles made from powdered marsh mallow root dates back to ancient times, when they were a sore throat treatment. Modern marshmallow, a favourite in hot chocolate and for toasting over a campfire, is a very different concoction. It no longer contains extracts from the herb, and consists simply of boiled sugar syrup combined with eggwhites and gelatine.

Marjoram & oregano

The Greeks called these fragrant-leafed herbs 'Brightness of the Mountain'. Their strong, warm aromatic taste characterises the cuisines of the Mediterranean.

∙∙∙

Latin name *Origanum* sp. Lamiaceae
Parts used Leaves, flowers

Sweet marjoram (*Origanum marjorana*)

 Gardening

More than 30 species of *Origanum* occur in the Mediterranean and the Middle East. Confusingly, marjoram and oregano are common names that are often used interchangeably.

Sweet or knot marjoram (*O. marjorana* syn. *Marjorana hortensis*) has grey-green leaves with a mouth-watering fragrance. Although usually treated as an annual, it is a short-lived perennial in mild climates.

Pot marjoram or Turkish oregano (*O. onites*) is a quite cold-tender, strongly aromatic species from Greece.

Common oregano (*O. vulgare*) contains six subspecies. *O. vulgare* subsp. *vulgare* is the mild-flavoured wild marjoram with clustered heads of pink flowers and deep burgundy bracts that attract bees, but lacks any appreciable flavour. It is often sold as 'oregano'. Cultivars of *O. vulgare* subsp. *vulgare* include the very attractive golden oregano, 'Aureum', sometimes sold as 'golden marjoram', which makes a superb aromatic groundcover for full sun, and 'Jim Best', which is a vigorous gold and green variegated variety. *O. pulchellum* is a name attached to forms of *O. vulgare* with purple bracts.

Greek oregano (*O. vulgare* subsp. *hirtum*) has a deliciously strong fragrance. The very mildly aromatic *O. vulgare* subsp. *virens* and *O. vulgare* subsp. *viridulum* are both given the common name of wild marjoram.

Lebanese oregano, Syrian hyssop or white oregano (*O. syriacum*) forms a tender perennial subshrub with grey-green foliage. Ezov, the biblical hyssop, was almost certainly *O. syriacum*.

Origanum sp.

Russian oregano (*O. vulgare* subsp. *gracile*) has an aroma that is similar to Greek oregano.

- **Growing** *Origanum* species are found in the wild in sunny, well-drained and often stony places. They thrive in full sun and are stronger flavoured if grown with tough love. Raise from seed in spring. Once the plants are established, do not overwater them. Cut back old growth in spring.
- **Harvesting and storing** You can harvest the foliage fresh but the flavour is enhanced if you dry it in bunches in a dark, dry, warm, well-ventilated place for several days. When dry and crisp, rub the leaves off the stems and store in an airtight container.

🌿 Herbal medicine

Origanum vulgare. Parts used: leaves, flowers. An infusion of the herb is considered a useful remedy for feverish conditions and also for treating coughs, colds and influenza due to its ability to improve the removal of phlegm from the lungs and relax the bronchial muscles.

Traditionally, oregano is also regarded as a herb for the gut; taken as a mild tea, it helps to relieve flatulence and improve digestion. It also has a soothing effect and may aid sleep.

For the safe and appropriate medicinal use of these two herbs, consult a healthcare professional. Do not use these herbs in greater than culinary quantities or the essential oils of these herbs internally or externally if you are pregnant or breastfeeding.

🌿 Cooking

Oregano has a more pungent scent than marjoram, with a stronger flavour. The hotter and drier the climate, the more aroma and flavour a variety will have.

Sweet marjoram is the type used in cooking. Its aroma is damaged by heat, so use it in uncooked or lightly cooked dishes, or add it at the end. Leaves and

Za'atar

Za'atar is an Arabic term for a number of aromatic herbs, often varying according to the region and also the local flora. While the term most often refers to origanums, za'atar species also include conehead thyme (*Thymbra capitata*), za'atar hommar (*T. spicata*), true thyme (*Thymus* sp.) and *Satureja* species such as *S. cuneifolia* and *S. thymbra*. The seasoning mixture called 'za'atar' usually includes toasted sesame seeds and coarse salt, and is used on vegetable and meat dishes and also sprinkled on bread before baking.

flowering tops add flavour to marinades, bastes for poultry, dressings, salads, soups and stuffings. You can also use sweet marjoram in herb butter and cheese spreads and to flavour oil and vinegar.

Oregano is a more robust herb and can withstand longer cooking. It is used to flavour sausages, salamis and pizzas, and is often used dried rather than fresh. Leaves and flowers are infused for tea.

Both herbs go well with lemon, garlic, onion, wine, meats, fish, salads, Greek and Italian dishes, beans, eggplant, capsicum and tomato-based dishes and sauces. They are also used in commercial mixed herbs.

For a relaxing soak, tie a tablespoonful each of dried sweet marjoram and oatmeal into a piece of cheesecloth and drop it into the bathwater.

Thyme and oregano soufflés

60 g butter

2 tablespoons plain flour

1⅓ cups (330 ml) milk

1 cup (125 g) grated strong cheddar

¼ teaspoon cayenne pepper

4 large eggs, separated

2 teaspoons finely chopped fresh thyme

2 teaspoons finely chopped fresh oregano

2 tablespoons finely chopped fresh parsley

2 tablespoons fruit chutney

1 Preheat oven to 200°C. Lightly oil four x 1-cup (250 ml) ramekins. Melt butter in small saucepan over low heat. Using wooden spoon, fold in flour and stir continuously for about 1 minute. Remove from heat.

2 Gradually add milk, stirring until smooth. Return pan to medium heat, stirring until mixture thickens and thickly coats back of spoon. Fold in cheese and cayenne pepper. Transfer mixture to large bowl, cover with plastic wrap; and leave to cool. When mixture is cool, stir through egg yolks and herbs.

3 In clean, small bowl, beat eggwhites until soft peaks form. Lightly fold eggwhites into soufflé mixture, just until white streaks are not visible. Do not overmix.

4 Place ½ tablespoon chutney in each ramekin. Divide soufflé mixture among ramekins, taking care not to mix in chutney. Run a small spatula around each rim to shape the top of soufflés. Place ramekins on an oven tray.

5 Bake soufflés 20 minutes, or until risen and golden. Serve at once.

SERVES 4

Meadowsweet

With its fragrant flowers, meadowsweet was a popular strewing herb in medieval times, and a favourite of Elizabeth I, who ordered it used in her bedchamber.

Meadowsweet (*Filipendula ulmaria*)

Latin name *Filipendula ulmaria* syn. *Spiraea ulmaria* Rosaceae
Also known as Bridewort, lady of the meadow, meadow queen, queen of the meadow
Parts used Flowers, leaves

Gardening

Meadowsweet bears dense, frothy, clusters of almond-scented, creamy white flowers in summer. The leaves are sweetly aromatic when crushed. The plant occurs in moist meadows and around fresh water, and is widely distributed across Asia and Europe.

Ornamental but herbally active varieties include the particularly desirable double-flowered 'Flore Pleno'; 'Grandiflora', with large flowers; 'Aurea', with golden foliage; and 'Variegata', with cream-variegated leaves. Dropwort (*F. vulgaris*), a closely related plant with similar flowers, was once used as a diuretic.

• **Growing** Hardy meadowsweet will grow in full sun, provided the soil is very moist. Sow seed in autumn, or propagate by division in spring. Every 3 or 4 years, lift and divide meadowsweet in autumn.

• **Harvesting and storing** Cut and dry flowers when in full bloom and use fresh for culinary use, or dried for herbal use. Harvest and dry leaves at the same time.

Meadowsweet was once used in garlands for brides and as a strewing herb at weddings.

Herbal medicine

Filipendula ulmaria syn. *Spiraea ulmaria*. Parts used: flowers, leaves. Meadowsweet is an important digestive remedy for conditions of the gut associated with inflammation and excess acidity. It has a balancing effect on acid production in the stomach as well as a soothing effect on the upper digestive tract. Infuse 4 to 6 dried leaves and flower tops in boiling water; drink 3 cups per day.

Meadowsweet contains aspirin-like compounds that can also help to bring down fevers, so the herb is often recommended for the treatment of colds and flu.

Do not use meadowsweet if you are pregnant or you are breastfeeding.

Cooking

The flowers are used to flavour jams, stewed fruits and mead as well as the non-alcoholic Norfolk Punch.

The source of aspirin

In 1827, salicin was isolated from meadowsweet's salicylate-containing leaves, then synthesised to acetyl salicylic acid (aspirin) by Felix Hoffman in Germany in 1899. His employer, Bayer A G, named the drug aspirin after an old botanical name for meadowsweet, *Spirea ulmaria*. The herb is considered less irritating to the stomach than the purified drug.

Mint

While everyone is familiar with spearmint and common mint, the amazing range of flavours and fragrances of mints also includes apple, chocolate, lime and ginger.

Variegated apple mint (*M. suaveolens* 'Variegata')

Latin name *Mentha* sp. Lamiaceae
Part used Leaves

Gardening

Spearmint (*Mentha spicata*) has spikes of lavender-coloured flowers.

Curly spearmint (*M. spicata* var. *crispa*) has fluted and curled foliage with a true spearmint scent. The large and slightly crinkly-leafed variety, 'Kentucky Colonel', is close to the common garden mint of Australia and England.

Spearmint (*Mentha spicata*)

Peppermint (*M.* x *piperita*) is a virtually sterile natural hybrid of water mint (*M. aquatica*) and spearmint (*M. spicata*). Varieties include 'Grapefruit' and the dark-leaved and quite delicious 'Chocolate' mint.

Water mint (*M. aquatica*) has a strong peppermint-like scent. The best-known variety is 'Eau de Cologne' or 'Bergamot', with a strong true scent of eau de cologne.

Apple or pineapple mint (*M. suaveolens*) is a fruit-scented species with finely hairy leaves.

Woolly or Bowle's mint (*M.* x *villosa* var. *alopecuroides*) is a vigorous, tall-growing species with broadly oval furred leaves.

Pennyroyal (*M. pulegium*) is a creeping mint that forms dense mats. Its small smooth leaves are powerfully hot mint-scented and the inflorescences have clusters of lavender flowers.

Corsican mint (*M. requinii*) is a strongly mint-scented ornamental that forms a dense groundcover of tiny leaves, well-suited to moist areas and large pots.

Rau ram (*Persicaria odorata* syn. *Polygonum odoratum*) is an easily grown perennial ideal for pot culture. Although not of the mint family, it is also called Vietnamese mint and is used in Asian cooking. Its pointed, lance-shaped leaves are green marked with deep brown and burgundy.

• Growing The ideal conditions are moist, rich soil and half to full sun. You can easily propagate mints from cuttings or by dividing clumps.

Pennyroyal (*M. pulegium*)

Peppermint (*Mentha* x *piperita*)

• **Harvesting and storing** Mints dry well in a warm, airy place away from direct sunlight. Store crumbled leaves in an airtight container. Harvest foliage to use fresh as required.

Herbal medicine

Mentha x *piperita*. Part used: leaves. Peppermint can help to relieve indigestion, nausea, gas and cramping. It can also help ease the symptoms of irritable bowel syndrome, including diarrhoea, constipation, bloating and abdominal pain, especially when taken as enteric-coated peppermint oil capsules.

Topically, peppermint essential oil has a pain-relieving effect, which can help alleviate the discomfort of joint and muscle pain and headaches. When it is inhaled, it can also help to reduce feelings of nausea and act as a nasal decongestant.

For the safe and appropriate medicinal use of peppermint, consult a healthcare professional. Do not use peppermint in greater than culinary quantities, and do not use the essential oil, if you are pregnant or breastfeeding.

Around the home

• Both peppermint and pennyroyal (*M. pulegium*) are natural insect repellents.
• Sprinkle cotton-wool balls with peppermint essential oil and leave them where rodents enter.

• Add a few drops of peppermint essential oil to a damp rag and wipe over benches and cupboard interiors to deter ants and cockroaches.
• To deter fleas, sprinkle dried pennyroyal under your dog's bedding or put a spot of oil on its collar. But don't use pennyroyal on cats or pregnant dogs, as it is toxic.
• To make a personal insect repellent, mix 1 part lavender, 1 part eucalyptus, 1 part peppermint essential oils with 3 parts unscented moisturiser or sweet almond oil, and rub into the skin.

Rau ram or Vietnamese mint (*Persicaria odorata*)

🌿 Natural beauty

Peppermint's pain-relieving effects make it a popular treatment for foot baths to soothe tired and aching feet. Peppermint oil is also an ingredient in cooling lotions for feet.

Peppermint foot scrub

Refresh your feet with this easy and effective scrub. Peppermint cools and deodorises and sugar buffs away dead skin.

1 tablespoon coarse-ground oatmeal

1 tablespoon polenta

1 tablespoon sugar

2 teaspoons dried peppermint leaves

1 tablespoon natural yogurt

juice of 1 lemon

5 drops peppermint essential oil

1 Combine oatmeal, polenta, sugar and peppermint leaves in a bowl.

2 Add yogurt, lemon juice and oil; mix to form a gritty paste.

3 To use, sit on the edge of the bath tub and massage mixture into feet, paying particular attention to heels and soles. Rinse and dry thoroughly and follow with a rich moisturiser.

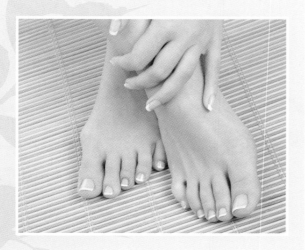

Mint jelly

500 g green apples, cored
  and roughly chopped

15 g roughly chopped fresh mint

1½ cups (375 ml) white wine vinegar

500 g jam-setting sugar

15 g finely chopped fresh mint, extra

Place apples, mint and vinegar in medium saucepan; cook, uncovered, until apples are very tender. Purée apples; drain through a sieve (don't push them through, but allow the liquid to run through so jelly doesn't become cloudy). Return liquid to saucepan; add sugar. Return to the boil, boiling for 10 minutes. Remove from heat, stir through extra mint. Pour into clean container; refrigerate 6 hours, or until set. Makes about 2 cups (600 g).

🌿 Cooking

Lovely though its flavour is, fresh mint can overwhelm milder flavours and is best used with a light hand. Dried mint is less assertive and is favoured in eastern Mediterranean and Arab countries.

In general, mint does not complement other herbs well, except parsley, thyme, marjoram, sage, oregano and coriander. It goes well with yogurt, and is used in Vietnamese food and in some Indian dishes. The coriander and lemon taste of Vietnamese mint is refreshing in salads.

Spearmint is the ordinary garden mint, and the most common culinary type. It is a classic flavouring for roast lamb and its accompaniments, and also goes well with potatoes, peas and salads.

Peppermint has a particularly strong flavour and aroma. It makes a pleasant digestive tea. The oil is used in ice-cream, confectionery and liqueurs.

Herb-crusted leg of lamb

2 tablespoons chopped fresh parsley

1 tablespoon chopped fresh rosemary, or 1 teaspoon dried
rosemary, crumbled

1 tablespoon chopped fresh thyme, or 1 teaspoon dried
thyme, crumbled

1 tablespoon chopped fresh mint, or 1 teaspoon dried
mint, crumbled

1 tablespoon olive oil

1 tablespoon balsamic vinegar

1 tablespoon dijon mustard

1 teaspoon sea salt

$1/2$ teaspoon freshly ground black pepper

1 whole leg of lamb (about 3 kg)

2 cloves garlic, cut into thin slivers

1 Preheat oven to 230°C. In a small bowl, combine all ingredients except the lamb and garlic.

2 Place lamb, fat side up, on a rack in a shallow roasting pan. With a small sharp knife, cut twelve slits, each 1 cm long and 1 cm deep, into the top of the lamb, 5 cm apart. Insert garlic slivers in each slit, pushing them into the meat.

3 Evenly spread herb mixture over the lamb. Roast, uncovered, for 15 minutes. Reduce oven temperature to 180°C; and roast, uncovered, a further 1¼ hours.

4 Remove lamb from oven and transfer to a carving board; cover loosely with foil. Allow to rest for 15–20 minutes before carving.

SERVES 8

Nettle

Nettles make their presence painfully obvious. As the famous 17th-century herbalist Culpeper noted, they 'may be found by feeling, in the darkest night'.

Latin name *Urtica dioica* Lamiaceae
Parts used Leaves, roots

🍃 Gardening

The stinging nettle (*Urtica dioica*) is a cold-tolerant herbaceous perennial growing to 1.2 m, with coarsely toothed, oval leaves armed with stinging hairs. Tiny green male and female flowers are borne on separate plants. The spreading roots are yellow. The young leaves are rich in minerals (particularly potassium, calcium, silicon and iron) and also contain vitamin C.

Nettles are a valuable food supply for the caterpillar stage of a number of butterfly species, and for the gardener-friendly larvae of ladybirds.

Always wear rubber gloves when handling nettles.

Classified into five subspecies, all of which have similar uses, *U. dioica* is indigenous to much of the temperate northern hemisphere. As an introduced plant, it is widespread in the temperate southern hemisphere.

● **Growing** Nettles prefer full sun to light shade and thrive in a rich, moist soil that is high in nitrogen. Plant seed in spring or, if you are brave, by division of plants in spring. Note that nettles can become invasive plants.

● **Harvesting and storing** In addition to spring picking, harvest in midsummer and again in autumn, and always wear gloves to protect your hands. Dig up the roots in autumn and air-dry them with the tops out of direct sunlight.

Nettle (*Urtica dioica*)

🍃 Herbal medicine

Urtica dioica. Parts used: Leaves, roots. Nettle leaf is a traditional blood-purifying remedy. It has a gentle diuretic effect and encourages the removal of toxins from the body. It is used medicinally to treat arthritic conditions and certain skin disorders such as eczema, which some herbalists believe can benefit from a detoxifying action.

The leaf is also associated with anti-allergic properties, and herbalists often prescribe it for symptoms of hay fever and skin rashes.

Modern research has shown that nettle root may inhibit overgrowth of prostate tissue, and clinical trials have provided some compelling evidence that therapeutic use of the root may improve the urinary symptoms associated with disorders of the prostate gland, such as frequent urination and weak flow.

For the safe and appropriate use of nettle, consult your healthcare professional. Do not use nettle in greater than culinary doses if you are pregnant or you are breastfeeding.

Relieve the discomfort of nettle stings by rubbing them with ice or the leaves of dock.

🍃 Cooking

The young leaves were once widely used in the spring diet to revitalise the body after winter. For culinary purposes, use leaf tips from plants less than 10 cm high, as these have yet to develop the stinging compounds. Nettle leaves may be cooked as a vegetable, in similar ways to spinach, or added to soups or to vegetable, egg or meat dishes. A tisane can be made from the leaves. Do not eat nettles raw; also note that older leaves are high in calcium oxalate and should not be eaten at all.

Cornish yarg

A handmade semi-hard cheese with a creamy taste, Cornish yarg is wrapped in nettle leaves after pressing and brining. The leaves are carefully arranged by hand to form a pleasing pattern and also to attract natural moulds in various colours that aid in the ripening process, adding a subtle mushroom taste. Remove yarg from the refrigerator about an hour before serving.

Nettle soup

Wearing gloves, pick tender young tips in spring, before they flower. Wash well and remove tough stalks.

1 tablespoon olive oil
1 white onion, diced
¼ cup (50 g) uncooked long-grain white rice
4 cups (1 litre) chicken stock
500 g nettle tops, chopped

Heat oil in saucepan; cook onion 5 minutes, until softened. Add rice, stock and nettles. Bring to the boil. Reduce heat and simmer 15 minutes until rice is tender. Purée soup in a blender and season to taste with salt and black pepper. Serves 4.

Parsley

Native to the southeastern Mediterranean, parsley was once used as fodder for the chariot horses of the ancient Greeks. It is a popular herb for growing at home.

Latin name *Petroselinum* sp. Apiaceae/Umbelliferae
Parts used Leaves, stalks, roots, seeds

Gardening

Parsley is a biennial crop, forming a dense rosette of leaves in the first year and flowering in its second summer, when the foliage becomes bitter.

There are three distinct types of parsley. Probably the most familiar is curly parsley (*P. crispum* var. *crispum*). The plain-leaf types, known as Italian or French or flat-leaf parsley (*P. crispum* var. *neapolitanum*), have flat leaf segments. In Italy, the true Italian parsley is considered to be 'Catalagno', which is usually listed elsewhere as 'Giant Italian'. Hamburg or turnip-rooted parsley (*P. crispum* var. *tuberosum*) is grown more for its delicately flavoured taproot than its leaves, although they can also be used.

• **Growing** Parsley prefers full morning sun to partial shade, and well-composted, well-drained but moist soil. It is grown only from seed and takes 3 to 8 weeks to germinate. You can speed up this process by soaking the seed in warm water overnight before planting. Transplant seedlings into the garden (or thin seedlings sown directly into the garden) to around 25 cm apart. Parsley self-seeds under suitable conditions. Water regularly or parsley will flower ('bolt') in its first season. Cutting out the emerging flowering stalks will frustrate this process to some extent.

• **Harvesting and storing** New growth comes from the centre of the stem, so harvest leaves from around the outside of plants. Wrap in a plastic bag and store in the freezer. Parsley is not a good herb for drying, as it loses much of its flavour. Collect seeds when pale brown. They ripen progressively from the outside of the inflorescence inward. Hang bunches of ripening seed heads upside-down inside paper bags. Harvest the roots at the end of the second season and air dry them.

Curly parsley (*Petroselinum crispum* var. *crispum*, pot) and flat-leaf parsley (*Petroselinum crispum* var. *neapolitanum*)

Country folk once said that only people who were wicked were able to grow lush parsley.

Herbal medicine

Petroselinum crispum var. *crispum*. Parts used: leaves, roots, seeds. The leaves are a good source of vitamin C, and both the leaf and root are well-known for their diuretic effects in the body. Parsley has been used to treat fluid retention, urinary tract disorders and arthritic conditions of the joints.

Parsley has a calming effect on the gut, alleviating flatulence and colic, and also a gentle stimulatory action, encouraging appetite and improving digestion.

For the safe and appropriate medicinal use of parsley, consult your healthcare professional. Do not use parsley in greater than culinary quantities if you're pregnant or you are breastfeeding.

Cooking

Flat-leaf parsley is generally considered to have the best flavour, while curly parsley has a pleasing crunchy texture. Use either as a garnish or in salads, egg and vegetable dishes and sauces.

Parsley is essential to many traditional flavouring mixtures, particularly in French cooking. Bouquet garni,

Emerald risotto

For a delicious and attractive emerald green herb risotto, cook a classic risotto recipe using arborio rice, chicken or vegetable stock and white wine, but add a handful of chopped baby spinach leaves when the rice is almost cooked. Once the rice is fully cooked (it should be a creamy, dropping consistency), stir in a generous amount of finely chopped fresh parsley and coriander. Season to taste.

a small bunch of pungent fresh herbs for slow cooking, is most often comprised of a bay leaf, sprigs of parsley and sprigs of thyme. Other mixes include chermoula and persillade (see *page 132*).

The edible root of Hamburg parsley is used in soups and stews and can be roasted or boiled in the same way as other root vegetables.

Rabbit's remedy

According to Greek myth, parsley sprang from the blood of a Greek hero, Archemorus, the forerunner of death, while English folklore has it that parsley seeds go to the Devil and back seven times before they germinate, referring to the fact that they can be slow to sprout. It is also claimed that only witches can grow it. On a more lighthearted note, however, parsley is traditionally a curative, a fact that Beatrix Potter weaves into *The Tale of Peter Rabbit* when Peter eats too much in Farmer McGregor's vegetable patch: 'First he ate some lettuce and some broad beans, then some radishes, and then, feeling rather sick, he went to look for some parsley.'

Parsley sauces

Parsley is cultivated in temperate climates throughout the world and is one of the most popular herbs for growing at home. It features in the herb mixes and sauces of many cuisines.

Persillade

This combination of chopped fresh parsley and garlic is classic French. It gives a great flavour boost to a dish if

added just at the very end of the cooking process. It can also be used as a garnish.

Use ½ cup parsley to 2 cloves garlic. Vary it with the addition of lemon zest or anchovies; tarragon or thyme can be used in place of parsley.

Chermoula

A Moroccan herb and spice mixture, chermoula is used as a marinade for meat, poultry and fish. It can also be applied as a paste, which forms a crust during cooking. Chermoula traditionally includes a mixture of fresh coriander and parsley, but the combination of spices can vary.

Combine ½ cup each finely chopped fresh coriander and parsley with 1 small finely chopped red onion, 2 crushed garlic cloves, 1 teaspoon each ground cumin, paprika, turmeric and chilli powder, ½ cup (125 ml) olive oil and 2 tablespoons lemon juice.

Chimichurri sauce

Try this Argentinian sauce with grilled meat. It can also be used as a marinade.

In a jar, combine 6 garlic cloves, 2 tablespoons fresh oregano leaves and a handful of parsley leaves, all finely chopped. Add 1 tablespoon chopped red onion, a pinch of dried red chilli flakes, 1 teaspoon ground black pepper, 150 ml olive oil, ½ cup (125 ml) red wine and salt, to taste. Seal jar, shake well. Leave 4 hours for the flavours to develop.

Tabbouleh beef wraps

4 large pita, halved

8 thin slices rare roast beef

4 slices Swiss-style cheese, halved

8 cherry tomatoes, quartered

1 avocado, peeled and sliced

2 tablespoons hummus

Tabbouleh

200 g burghul or cracked wheat

2 medium tomatoes, peeled, seeded
  and finely chopped

1 Lebanese or small cucumber,
  finely diced

5 tablespoons finely chopped fresh mint

3/4 cup (25 g) finely chopped fresh
  flat-leaf parsley

2 spring onions, finely chopped

2 tablespoons olive oil

juice of 1 lemon

1 To make tabbouleh, soak burghul
   in hot water 15 minutes. Drain;
   squeeze out excess water. Combine
   with remaining ingredients in
   medium bowl, and season to taste.

2 Fill pita halves with tabbouleh, beef,
   cheese, tomatoes, avocado and
   hummus. Serve at once.

SERVES 4

Parsley is a key ingredient in tabbouleh, a traditional Middle Eastern salad.

Passionflower

The passionflower gets its name from the Passion of Christ: the three stigmas symbolise the nails, the fringe the crown of thorns, the five stamens the wounds, and the petals the faithful Apostles.

....

Latin name *Passiflora incarnata* Passifloraceae
Also known as Maypops, purple passionflower, wild apricot, wild passionflower
Parts used Dried aerial parts (especially leaves), ripe fruits, flowers

Gardening

There are about 400 species of passionfruit. Many are ornamental, tendrilled climbers; some produce delicious fruit. Most require warm-temperate to tropical conditions, although *P. incarnata* is one of the most tolerant of cooler conditions.

A common wildflower in the southern United States, it was used as a tonic by Native Americans, and was first noted by a Western doctor in 1783. The fragrant large flowers are lavender-coloured, with a white centre and a deeper purple, thread-like corona. The fruits, ovoid yellow berries when ripe, are about 5 cm long.
• **Growing** It prefers a light, acidic soil and a warm, sunny position. Provide a trellis or other support, and mulch plants well.
• **Harvesting and storing** Harvest the aerial parts in mid- to late summer and air-dry for medicinal use. For culinary use, pick the fruits at the 'dropping' stage.

Herbal medicine

Passiflora incarnata. Part used: leaves. Medicinally, passionflower can be of benefit in conditions in which nervous tension and stress are prominent factors, and is used traditionally to treat anxiety disorders. This herb has a calming effect on the mind and body, and is used for insomnia in adults and children, especially when sleep troubles are accompanied by anxiety. To treat insomnia, infuse 2 g of dried passionflower leaves in boiling water and take 1 cup an hour before bedtime. For anxiety, take the same dose twice or more during the day.

Do not use passionflower if you are pregnant or you are breastfeeding.

Cooking

The seeds and pulp of ripe fruits have a tangy flavour, and are eaten raw or used in fruit salads and other desserts, curds, jams and jellies. The 'Hurricane' cocktail is made with passionfruit syrup, rum and lime juice.

Passionfruit cordial

Spoon the pulp of 8 passionfruit into a mixing bowl; you need about 3/4 cup (180 ml) pulp. Add 1 teaspoon vanilla extract, 1 cup (230 g) caster sugar and 1/4 cup (60 ml) lemon juice; stir well. Pour into a sterilised airtight bottle and refrigerate. Keeps for 1 week. To serve, pour into a jug and add 4 cups (1 litre) chilled soda water. Serves 8.

To Spanish missionaries in South America the structure of this strikingly attractive flower represented the Passion of Christ.

Passionflower (*Passiflora incarnata*)

Peony

Peonies have been cultivated in eastern Asia for more than 2000 years. The roots were used medicinally and the blooms were the favoured flower of Chinese emperors.

Latin name *Paeonia lactiflora* syn. *P. albiflora*, *P. officinalis*, *P. suffruticosa* syn. *P. moutan* Paeoniaceae
Also known as Bai shao, Chinese peony, white peony (*P. lactiflora*)
Parts used Roots, flowers

Gardening

The Chinese peony (*P. lactiflora*) is a herbaceous perennial that bears very large, scented flowers, which in the wild are white and single. Cultivated plants can be red, pink or purple and are usually double.

The tree peony (*P. suffruticosa*), found from western China to Bhutan, forms a branched upright shrub. The flowers are very large and slightly fragrant.

Common peony (*P. officinalis*) is a herbaceous perennial with large flowers that are single, fragrant, and usually purple-crimson.

• **Growing** Peonies prefer cold winters and a deep, rich, moist soil. Sow seed in autumn. You can also divide

Peony (*Paeonia lactiflora*)

plants in late autumn or early spring. Peonies require heavy feeding, and their roots resent disturbance. Remove dead wood in spring.

The peony is named after Paeon, physician to the Greek gods.

Herbal medicine

Paeonia lactiflora. Part used: roots. In traditional Chinese medicine, white peony root nourishes the blood and is a remedy for the treatment of conditions of the female reproductive system. Herbalists prescribe it, often with licorice, to regulate the menstrual cycle and relieve pain.

White peony can also have a relaxing effect on muscles, and it may have a blood pressure-lowering effect. Traditionally it has also been used to ease muscle cramps, relieve night sweats and treat angina.

For the safe and appropriate use of white peony, consult your healthcare professional. Do not take white peony if you are pregnant or breastfeeding.

Cooking

The flowers of *P. officinalis* are used to scent tea, and the seeds were once used as a spice.

Gender bias

The old herbalists recognised two different leaf forms of *P. officinalis* as 'male' and 'female' peonies, which were used for male and female complaints, respectively. The 'female' peony had leafier foliage, scented dark purple flowers and black seeds, while the 'male' peony had purple-red flowers and black and crimson seeds.

Perilla

Spicily aromatic perilla is used fresh in salads and for pickling and flavouring. Colourful and curly-leafed forms are popular as an ornamental bedding annual.

Latin name *Perilla frutescens* syn. *P. ocimoides*
Lamiaceae
Also known as Beafsteak plant, Chinese basil, shiso
Parts used Leaves, flower spikes, seed

Gardening

Perilla is a branched annual that grows to about 1.2 m. Its leaves vary in colour from green to red and purple. The leaf edges may be curled (a form previously called *P. crispum*); the tiny white to purple flowers are borne in dense spikes about 10 cm long. The varieties 'Green Cumin' and 'Purple Cumin' have cumin- and cinnamon-scented leaves. 'Aojiso' has green ginger-scented leaves, often used with sushi. The large-leafed 'Kkaennip' or Korean perilla is used in salads and food wraps, and the seeds for flavouring.

Perilla (*Perilla frutescens*)

Japanese cuisine

In Japan the fresh red leaves of perilla are used in salads or as a garnish or wrapping for dishes such as sushi. The leaves are also used to colour and flavour pickled plums (pictured) and ginger, while the seeds are sprouted for use in salads, or pickled as a condiment for Japanese dishes. Different varieties of perilla are also used in Indonesian, Vietnamese and Korean cuisine.

• **Growing** Perilla flourishes in moist, well-drained soils enriched with compost. Plant seed in spring.
• **Harvesting and storing** Harvest leaves in summer and use fresh or dried. Harvest flower spikes when they are fully developed, and the seed in autumn.

Herbal medicine

Perilla frutescens. Parts used: leaves, seeds. Perilla is commonly prescribed for respiratory conditions, including colds and coughs, and to ease symptoms caused by poor digestive function, such as lack of appetite, nausea and bloating. Oral preparations of perilla are prescribed to ease hay fever symptoms. Take up to 9 g of dried leaf per day in tablet or capsule form.

Don't use perilla in greater that culinary quantities if you are pregnant or breastfeeding.

Cooking

The red variety of perilla is more often used for culinary purposes than the green. (Note that excessive handling can cause dermatitis.) The leaves of *P. frutescens* contain a compound that is 2000 times sweeter than sugar and is used as an artificial sweetener in Japan.

Plantain

Although common plantain is considered a weed of lawns by many gardeners, it has long been valued in folk medicine, and continues to find herbal uses.

· ·

Latin name *Plantago major, P. lanceolata, P. psyllium* Plantaginaceae
Also known as Greater plantain, rat-tail plantain (*P. major*)
Parts used Leaves (*P. major, P. lanceolata*); seeds, seed husks (*P. psyllium, P. ovata*)

🌿 Gardening

Common plantain (*P. major*) is a perennial with large leaves and spikes of tiny flowers. Psyllium (*P. psyllium*) is an annual with flowers that release tiny seeds.
· **Growing** *P. psyllium* and *P. ovata* prefer full sun and a well-drained soil. *P. major* prefers a moist situation with light shade. Plant seed in spring.
· **Harvesting and storing** Cut the leaves and dry them for herbal use, as required. Collect seed when ripe, as soon as the dew has dried, and dry them also.

🌿 Herbal medicine

Plantago lanceolata, P. major. Part used: leaves. Due to plantain's mucilaginous compounds, it has a soothing effect on the lungs, reducing inflammation and helping to remove catarrh. Plantain is also used for its healing effect on gastric ulcers, and can be used as a gargle for inflammatory conditions of the mouth and throat, and as an ointment it can be applied to cuts and bruises.

Plantago psyllium. Parts used: seeds, husks. Psyllium is an excellent bulk laxative. The soluble fibre contained in the seeds absorbs water, making bowel movements easier and more regular. As well, the fibre binds to cholesterol enabling it to be excreted from the body. Psyllium can be taken in tablet form, or a teaspoon of the powdered husk can be sprinkled on cereal or fruit once a day. Take every dose with a large glass of water.

For the safe and appropriate use of plantain and psyllium, consult a healthcare professional. Do not use these herbs if you are pregnant or breastfeeding.

A sacred herb

One of the Nine Sacred Herbs of the Anglo-Saxons, plantain was believed to cure headaches. The *Lacnunga*, a collection of medical texts written in the 11th or 12th century, relates this story of the god Woden: '…out of the worm sprang nine poisons. So Woden took his sword and changed it into nine herbs. These herbs did the wise lord create and sent them into the world for rich and poor, a remedy for all…'

Common plantain (*Plantago major*)

Poppy

Poppies have been grown for 5000 years, for medicinal, culinary and ornamental purposes. Opium poppy is the source of some of our most important pain killers.

Californian poppy (*Eschscholzia californica*)

Latin name *Papaver rhoeas, P. somniferum*; *Eschscholzia californica* Papaveraceae
Parts used Aerial parts (Californian poppy only); latex (opium poppy only)

🍃 Gardening

The opium poppy (*P. somniferum*) is a hardy annual that grows to about 1.2 m with large, coarse, toothed, silvery green foliage and tall flowering stems bearing four-petalled flowers that may be white, pink, lavender or red, followed by a globose capsule with an operculum that opens to scatter the ripe seed. The wall of the green capsule oozes bitter white latex when wounded.

Opium poppy cultivation is strictly controlled in many countries; however, a number of ornamental forms are widely grown, including the 19th-century red and white 'Danish Flag', double 'peony' forms and the very old 'Hen and Chickens', which has a ring of tiny flowers encircling each large flower.

The European annual red or field poppy (*P. rhoeas*) has four silken, bright red petals, sometimes with a black blotch in the centre. It was used to breed ornamental Shirley poppies.

Californian poppy (*Eschscholzia californica*), which is related to true poppies, is a heat- and drought-resistant annual, native to the western United States, with the subspecies *mexicana* extending south into the Sonoran Desert. The blue-green, finely divided leaves form a basal rosette and the many flower stalks bear single silken, four-petalled flowers in lemon to orange.

• **Growing** All poppies, including Californian poppy, require a well-drained soil and sunny position. To sow poppy seeds evenly during spring, mix them first with dry sand.

• **Harvesting and storing** Harvest and dry the petals immediately after the flowers fully open. Collect seed from ripe capsules and dry them.

🍃 Herbal medicine

Eschscholzia californica. Parts used: aerial parts. The aerial parts of Californian poppy were used by Native Americans as a pain killer, and have been incorporated into Western herbal medicine as a valuable pain-relieving and relaxing herb. It is used for treating insomnia, anxiety and over-excitability, and may be a useful remedy for aiding relaxation during times of tension and stress.

Poppies were once symbolic both of the Earth goddess and of Ceres, the goddess of cereals.

Californian poppy alleviates many types of pain, including headaches, nervous cramping of the bowel, and rheumatic and nerve pain.

Substances known as alkaloids are responsible for the plant's sedating and pain-killing properties, and are similar to those found in opium poppy, from which morphine and codeine are derived. However, the alkaloids that are found in Californian poppy have a far gentler therapeutic effect and are also regarded as non-habit forming.

Papaver rhoeas. Part used: petals. Despite being closely related to the opium poppy, the red or field poppy possesses none of its counterpart's potent narcotic effects. Instead, it is used as a reliable traditional remedy for soothing respiratory conditions that are associated with irritable coughing and the presence of catarrh. Red poppy is regarded as mildly sedating and can be useful for alleviating poor or disturbed sleep.

For the safe and appropriate use of Californian and red poppy, consult your healthcare professional. Do not use these herbs if you are pregnant or breastfeeding.

Poppy seeds, the source of poppy oil, are harmless flavourings for baked goods.

Cooking

Poppy seeds are not narcotic and are widely liked for their flavour and crunchy texture. They are popular in baked goods, such as breads, cakes, pastries, muffins and bagels. In India, the seeds are ground and used to thicken sauces. The seeds also feature in Jewish and German cooking.

Lemon poppy seed cake

1/3 (75 g) cup sugar

1 egg

3 tablespoons canola oil

3 tablespoons orange juice

1/2 teaspoon lemon essence

2/3 cup (100 g) plain flour

3/4 teaspoon baking powder

1/8 teaspoon salt

1 teaspoon poppy seeds

1/3 cup (40 g) icing sugar

2 tablespoons lemon juice

1 Preheat oven to 180°C. Grease and flour a 23 x 13 x 7 cm loaf tin.

2 In a small bowl, combine sugar, egg, oil, orange juice and lemon essence. Combine flour, baking powder and salt; add to egg mixture and mix well. Stir in poppy seeds.

3 Bake 30–35 minutes or until a skewer inserted into the centre comes out clean. Cool for 10 minutes before removing from pan to a wire rack to cool completely.

4 For a glaze, whisk icing sugar and lemon juice in a small bowl until smooth; drizzle over cake.

SERVES 6

Red or field poppy (*Papaver rhoeas*)

Remembrance Day

The seeds of the red or field poppy lie dormant until the ground is disturbed, most usually by agriculture, then germinate to bloom abundantly.

In the World War I battlefields around Flanders in northern Europe, red poppies flourished in the ravaged earth. In May 1915 Canadian medical officer John McCrae wrote the poem (right) the day after conducting the funeral service for a friend killed in action. Since 1918 red poppies have been a symbol of Armistice or Remembrance Day, 11 November.

In Flanders Fields

In Flanders fields the poppies blow
Between the crosses, row on row,
That mark our place; and in the sky
The larks, still bravely singing, fly
Scarce heard amid the guns below.

We are the dead. Short days ago
We lived, felt dawn, saw sunset glow,
Loved, and were loved, and now we lie
In Flanders fields.

Take up our quarrel with the foe
To you from failing hands we throw
The torch; be yours to hold it high.
If ye break faith with us who die
We shall not sleep, though poppies grow
In Flanders fields.

Lieutenant Colonel John McCrae, 1872–1918

On 11 November, Remembrance Day, wreaths of artificial field poppies are placed on war memorials in memory of the fallen.

Primrose & cowslip

Cowslips were once known as 'cowsloppes', as it was thought that they grew in cow droppings, Traditionally, it was said that if you nibbled cowslips you would see fairies.

Cowslip (*P. veris*)

Latin name *Primula vulgaris, P. veris* Primulaceae
Also known as Paigle (cowslip)
Parts used Leaves, flowers, roots

Gardening

Primrose (*P. vulgaris*) is a perennial with stalked, solitary flowers with a sweet, fresh fragrance rising from a rosette of leaves. The flowers are five-petalled and pale golden yellow (rarely white), with a central cleft in each petal. The foliage of cowslips (*P. veris*) closely resembles

Strewing herbs

In the Middle Ages, strewing herbs were used instead of, or mixed with, rushes or straw as a floor covering. They helped to mask unpleasant odours, deter household pests and, it was believed, protect against disease.

According to Thomas Tusser's *Five Hundred Good Points of Husbandry* (1573), the 21 strewing herbs comprised: 'Bassell [basil], Bawlme [lemon balm], Camamel [chamomile], Costemary [costmary], Cowsleps and paggles [cowslips], Daisies of all sorts, Sweet fennel, Germander, Hysop [hyssop], Lavender, Lavender spike, Lavender cotten [santolina], Marjorom, Mawdelin, Peny ryall [pennyroyal], Roses of all sorts, Red myntes, Sage, Tansey, Violets, Winter savery.'

that of primroses, but the smaller, golden yellow, sweetly scented flowers are borne in clusters at the top of each flowering stem, well above the leaves. According to the English herbalist John Gerard, writing in the 16th century, a tisane made from the flowers was drunk in the month of May to cure the 'frenzie'.

• **Growing** Primroses require a moist, rich soil and light shade, while cowslips prefer a well-drained drier site in full sun or light shade. Propagate cowslips and primroses by seed or by division. Break up any clumps and replant well-rooted divisions every 2 years.

• **Harvesting and storing** Gather leaves and flowers in spring to use fresh, and for use in preserves and wine. Before storing, air-dry flowers, leaves and roots (lifted in autumn).

Herbal medicine

Primula veris. Parts used: flowers, roots. Cowslip is associated with relaxing and sedative properties and is used to treat insomnia and restlessness as well as stress.

Cowslip is also traditionally used to alleviate catarrhal congestion and irritable coughs associated with some respiratory disorders, such as bronchitis.

For the safe and appropriate use of cowslip, consult a healthcare professional. Do not use cowslip if you are pregnant or breastfeeding.

Hang bunches of flower stems, with their stems straight, where warm air can circulate around them.

Purslane

In centuries past, purslane was believed a cure for 'blastings by lightning'. Now often considered a weed, it was once appreciated as a salad, pickle and sautéed vegetable.

Latin name *Portulaca oleracea* Portulacaceae
Parts used Leaves, stems

Gardening

Purslane is an annual that grows to about 7 cm high and up to 45 cm wide, with soft trailing branches and spoon-shaped, succulent green leaves with a slight crunchy texture. Purslane has been used as a food and a medicine in the Mediterranean basin, India and China.

- **Growing** Purslane prefers well-drained soils, growing in full sun to light shade. Plant the seeds in spring. During the growing season, trailing branches will root where they touch the ground; detach the rooted tips and plant them out. Keep the soil moist.
- **Harvesting and storing** Harvest fresh plants before flowering, or the flavour will deteriorate. Dry them for decoctions.

Purslane
(*Portulaca oleracea*)

Cooking

Purslane has a slightly sour, salty, lemony spinach flavour. It has been eaten for thousands of years in India, where it grows wild. Leaves are most commonly used, but the roots, flowers and seeds are also edible.

The plant contains mucilage, giving the palate a glutinous sensation and also serving to thicken such dishes as soups and sauces. Blanching reduces both the mucilage and the jelly-like leaf texture.

Purslane was popular in England in the Elizabethan era and is once again finding favour as a culinary herb. You can cook it in a similar manner to spinach. In French cooking, the fleshy leaves are used raw in salads, or they are cooked in equal amounts with sorrel to make the classic soup *bonne femme*. In Asia, purslane is used in stir-fries. Traditionally, Aboriginal Australians used the seeds to make seed cakes.

Purslane makes an excellent pickle, using wine or apple cider vinegar spiced with garlic, chilli and whole peppercorns.

Purslane strewn around a bed was once believed to ward off evil spirits.

Red clover

Red clover has been a forage and soil-improving crop since the Middle Ages. It is increasingly important as a medicinal herb, particularly for menopausal symptoms.

....

Latin name *Trifolium pratense* Fabaceae
Also known as Meadow honeysuckle, meadow trefoil, purple clover, wild clover
Parts used Flowers, young leaves

Red clover (*Trifolium pratense*)

Gardening

Red clover is a short-lived European perennial widely grown as a forage crop. In common with other clovers, nitrogen-fixing bacteria in its root nodules assimilate atmospheric nitrogen into the plant and significantly improve soil fertility. The plants form a creeping groundcover; the stalked flower spikes are dense and club-shaped, composed of many pink to purple pea flowers, which are rich in nectar.

Closely related species include lucerne or alfalfa (*Medicago sativa*), and fenugreek (*Trigonella foenum-graecum*). The latter is an important spice in Indian cooking. Medicinally, it is used under professional supervision to help manage blood glucose in patients with diabetes, and as a cholesterol-lowering agent.
- **Growing** Red clover prefers a well-drained, light soil, a cool to mild spring and full sunlight. Sow in spring.
- **Harvesting and storing** Harvest red clover up to 3 times in a growing season. Harvest the leaves when young; use the flowers fresh or dried.

Herbal medicine

Trifolium pratense. Parts used: flowers. Red clover flowers have been used, both internally and externally, as a remedy for the treatment of eczema and psoriasis, particularly in children. Taken as an infusion or syrup of the flowers, it also alleviates the coughing associated with respiratory conditions, such as bronchitis.

These days, the most common medicinal application for red clover centres around the use of isolated compounds known as isoflavones that come from the leaves and flowers. These compounds have been shown to possess mild oestrogenic activity, and clinical studies suggest that they can alleviate many of the symptoms associated with menopause. There is some evidence that red clover may also help maintain bone density.

For the safe and appropriate use of red clover, consult a healthcare professional. Do not use red clover if you are pregnant or breastfeeding.

The shamrock

In the teachings of St Patrick, the clover's trifoliate leaves (from the Latin *tri*, meaning 'three', and *folium*, 'leaf') symbolised the Holy Trinity — the doctrine that God is the Father, Son and Holy Spirit — and became the shamrock of Ireland. Although the Celtic harp is the official symbol of Ireland, the shamrock is the popular symbol of St Patrick's Day.

Rocket or arugula

Native to the Mediterranean basin and eastward to Turkey and Jordan, rocket has been popular as a salad green since Roman times for its peppery, smoky, meaty flavour.

....

Latin name *Eruca sativa* syn. *Eruca vesicaria* subsp. *sativa* Brassicaceae
Also known as Italian cress, Roman rocket, rucola, rugula
Parts used Leaves, flowers, seeds

Rocket or arugula (*Eruca sativa*)

Gardening

Rocket (*Eruca sativa*) is an annual plant resembling an open lettuce. Leaves are aromatic and peppery, and add considerable flavour to other salad greens, while the piquantly flavoured, four-petalled white flowers can be added to salads. Tall rocket or tumbling mustard (*Sisymbrium altissimum*), London rocket (*S. irio*) and Mediterranean rocket or smooth mustard (*S. erysimoides*) all have a peppery flavour. Plants sold as wild rocket or wild arugula or roquette sauvage are usually *Diplotaxis tenuifolia* syn. *Brassica tenuifolia*, a species with yellow flowers and leaves that resemble a more slender version of rocket.

Because of its use since the days of ancient Rome, this peppery-tasting herb is still sometimes called Roman rocket.

• **Growing** Plant rocket in full sun in the cooler months, but in midsummer provide some light shade. Rocket is quite unfussy otherwise, thriving in average garden soil. Wild arugula requires similar conditions. Sow rocket in successive plantings each month, from spring to autumn, as it tends to run to flower.

• **Harvesting and storing** Rocket leaves are best gathered before flowering, after which they become more bitter. Wash well and store it in the refrigerator in the same way as lettuce. Harvest flowers as required for fresh use and collect seeds when ripe.

Cooking

Rocket has a peppery flavour when grown in the cooler months, but a stronger, mustard-like taste if harvested in summer. It goes well with other salad leaves — a traditional Roman salad contains rocket, witlof, cos lettuce, tender mallow leaves, lavender and cheese.

Rapidly sauté or steam rocket for use in pasta and risotto dishes, stir-fries, soups and sauces, or to replace basil in pesto. Rocket needs only the briefest cooking. The ancient Romans used rocket seeds to flavour oil and to concoct aphrodisiacs. The seeds make excellent sprouts and are also pressed for oil.

High in vitamin C and iron, rocket stimulates the appetite and assists digestion.

Potato pizza with chicken and rocket

500 g small new potatoes, scrubbed

2 tablespoons olive oil

2 red onions, halved and very thinly sliced

75 g pancetta, diced

175 g button mushrooms, sliced

1 tablespoon fresh rosemary

2 ready-made pizza bases, each about 22 cm across

90 ml low-fat milk

250 g cooked skinless chicken breast, shredded

85 g rocket

2 tablespoons shaved parmesan

1 Preheat the oven to 220°C. Using a mandolin, a fine slicing disc in a food processor, or a very sharp knife, cut the potatoes into wafer-thin slices. Cook in a large saucepan of lightly salted boiling water for 1–2 minutes until just tender. Drain.

2 Heat the oil in the frying pan and gently fry onions and pancetta for 2–3 minutes. Add mushrooms and cook for a further 2 minutes. Add potatoes and rosemary, season with black pepper and very gently toss.

3 Place pizza bases on two lightly greased baking trays. Top with the potato mixture. Drizzle the milk over the topping. Bake for 15 minutes, until the potatoes are tender and golden.

4 Transfer pizzas to a chopping board. Cut into quarters and place two quarters on each plate. Equally divide the chicken among the pieces of pizza, then scatter the rocket and parmesan shavings over the top. Serve at once.

SERVES 4

Rose

The edible petals of herbal roses are used in conserves, salads and desserts, while the petals of some varieties yield the richly fragrant attar of roses used in perfumery.

....

Latin name *Rosa* sp. Rosaceae
Parts used Petals, rosehips

🌿 Gardening

Herbal roses, not modern ones — fragrant and beautiful though they are — are the roses of choice for cooking, fragrance and herbal medicines.

'Apothecary Rose'

The most famous herbal rose is *R. gallica* 'Officinalis', sometimes called the 'Rose of Miletus', the 'Rose of Provins', the 'Red Rose of Lancaster' and 'Champagne Rose' (see The Wars of the Roses, opposite page).

The 'Apothecary Rose' was cultivated in vast fields around the famous town of Provins, 50 km southeast of Paris, from the 13th to the 19th centuries. Unlike other roses, the fragrance in the petals is strongly retained after drying. The petals are tonic and astringent, and were used by many physicians, including the great Arab doctor Avicenna.

In Provins, the petals of 'Officinalis' were manufactured into conserves, jellies, syrups, cordials, pastilles, fragrant perfumes, salves, creams and candles, all products still favoured today.

'Officinalis' was grown in monastery gardens throughout Europe. The petals, either administered as a tea or a syrup, were used to treat the common cold, inflammation of the digestive tract and hysteria. A decoction was used to treat sprains, chapped lips and sore throats.

Other long-favoured roses for the herb garden include the Gallica roses 'Tuscany' ('Old Velvet'), 'Belle Isis', 'Duchesse de Montebello' and 'Belle de Crécy', together with the Centifolia rose 'Reine des Centfeuilles'.

Attar of roses

Today, the major producers of rose products and the fabulously expensive perfume concentrate attar (otto) of roses are Iran and Bulgaria. Both regions grow the Damask rose (*R.* x *damascena*), 'Ispahan' and 'Gloire de Guilan' being favoured in Iran and 'Kazanlik' syn. 'Trigintipetala' in Bulgaria. The area around Grasse in France still produces attar, derived mainly from the 'Old Cabbage Rose' (*R. centifolia*). A small amount comes from the Alba rose and the Damask rose 'Quatre Saisons'.

Rosehips

The single-flowered varieties of Rugosa rose (*R. rugosa*), with their abundant, repeat-flowering habit, and tolerance of cold and seaside locations, bear clusters of plum-sized hips that are excellent for use in syrups and teas. Rosehip oil, also known as *rose mosqueta*, is very rich in essential fatty acids and has multiple benefits for the skin. This oil, an anti-oxidant and astringent that contains flavonoids and carotenoids, is prepared from the hips of both *R. canina* and *R. eglanteria*.

The beautiful *Rosa canina* is a source of rosehip oil.

The Wars of the Roses

The 'Apothecary Rose', *Rosa gallica* 'Officinalis', may have been introduced from the Middle East into Western Europe by the Crusaders. In England, it became the symbol of the House of Lancaster in the Wars of the Roses (1455–1487). The opposing House of York adopted the ancient semi-double Alba rose, 'The White Rose of York' (*R. alba* 'Semi-plena'), while the Jacobites chose the fully double form, which became known as the Jacobite Rose (*R. alba* 'Plena'). At the end of the wars, Henry VII, the father of Henry VIII, combined them into the Tudor Rose, usually depicted as a double rose with white on red, one of the symbols of the House of Tudor.

• **Growing** The herbal roses prefer full sun, although the Alba roses are the most shade-tolerant of all roses. Most of the herbal roses flower only once a year but extremely abundantly over a month. 'Quatre Saisons' is repeat flowering. Rugosa roses are highly repeat flowering over a long season. All respond well to the incorporation of well-rotted compost, but avoid using modern fast-release fertilisers.

Old roses are very tough and need not be pruned or sprayed. If you wish to prune them for shaping, do so immediately after flowering ceases as they flower on ripe wood. Apply mulch in summer.

The varieties mentioned above recover rapidly from any attack and can be grown without sprays, while rugosa roses such as 'Frau Dagmar Hastrup' and 'Alba' are remarkably disease-resistant.

• **Harvesting and storing** Harvest herbal roses when the flowers have just opened, on sunny mornings as soon as the dew has dried. To dry, spread the flowers on flyscreen-covered frames out of direct sunlight. Harvest the hips (fruits) when fully coloured and slightly soft to the touch. Dry in the same way as the flowers. Store in a cool place.

Herbal medicine

Rosa canina. Part used: Rosehips. The hips of dog rose contain notable levels of vitamin C, and can be taken as a tea or syrup in winter to help fight off common colds and flus. In Britain during World War II wild rosehips were harvested to make rosehip syrup as a vitamin C supplement for children. Also, because of their slightly drying nature, rosehips have also been used to reduce symptoms of diarrhoea.

Medicinal preparations of rosehip, mainly in the powdered form, have been the focus of recent scientific research for the treatment of osteoarthritic conditions. The results of clinical trials suggest that it may reduce symptoms of pain and stiffness.

For the safe and appropriate medicinal use of rosehips, consult your healthcare professional Do not use rosehips in greater than culinary quantities if you're pregnant or breastfeeding, except under the supervision of a professional.

Rose oil was traditionally used to anoint British monarchs during the coronation ceremony.

Natural beauty

Rosewater distilled from the petals is a fragrant and mildly astringent tonic for the skin; it is especially useful for chapped skin and may also be used in soothing preparations for eye infections, such as conjunctivitis.

Rose essential oil has anti-ageing effects and may be used in preparations to soothe and heal dry and sensitive skins as well as to reduce the appearance of fine wrinkles.

Around the home

Use dried petals in Rose and lavender pot-pourri (see *page 97*) to place in bowls around your home.

Turkish delight

Rosewater, a by-product of the distilling process that makes rose oil from rose petals, is an important flavouring in Middle Eastern cooking. It is used for some Asian and Middle Eastern sweets, including Turkish delight, and the rasgullas and gulab jamuns of Indian cooking. Turkish delight is a sticky, jelly-like but firm sweet, made from starch and sugar. It is traditionally flavoured with rosewater and generously dusted with icing sugar; other flavours include lemon and mint. The confectionery was introduced to the West in the 19th century, when a British man, who was fond of it, shipped some home.

Cooking

The hips (fruits) and petals of some varieties of roses — including *R. canina*, *R.* x *damascena* and *R. gallica* — are edible. The petals can be crystallised and used for decoration, to make rose petal jam, crushed and added to flavour wines or (with the bitter 'heel' at the base of the petals removed) added to salads.

Rosehips are high in vitamin C and can be made into jams, jellies or a syrup that serves as a dietary supplement for babies.

Ras el hanout, the Moroccan spice blend, has many variations, some of which contain dried rose petals and flower buds.

Rose petal jelly

4 gelatine sheets (or 2 heaped teaspoons
  powdered gelatine)

2 cups (500 ml) sparkling wine

2/3 cup (145 g) caster sugar

1 tablespoon rosewater

18 small rose petals, carefully washed

raspberries and cream, to serve

1 Soak gelatine leaves in cold water to soften (about
   2–3 minutes).

2 Heat 1/2 cup (125 ml) sparkling wine and the sugar
   in large saucepan over medium heat, stirring until
   sugar dissolves.

3 Add gelatine leaves to sugar mixture, stirring to melt
   gelatine. Remove from heat to cool. Stir through
   remaining sparkling wine, rosewater and rose petals.

4 Pour mixture into individual glasses or a lightly oiled
   mould. Refrigerate at least 8 hours, or until set. Serve
   jelly with raspberries and cream.

SERVES 2

Rosemary

Few herbs are as widely grown and loved as rosemary. It plays many roles in the garden and the refreshing resinous flavour of its foliage is indispensable in cooking.

....

Latin name *Rosmarinus officinalis* Lamiaceae
Also known as Compass plant, dew of the sea, incensier, Mary's mantle
Parts used Leaves, flowering tops

Gardening

Rosmarinus means 'dew of the sea', and in the wild this evergreen herb is most commonly found growing on sea cliffs around the Mediterranean. Despite their

Scholars in ancient Greece wore rosemary garlands when sitting exams to enhance their memory and improve their concentration.

different forms and colours, all the rosemary varieties offered in nurseries belong to one species, *R. officinalis*. Rosemary flowers vary from pale to rich blue, violet, mauve, pink or white. The form varies, from rounded bushes suitable for hedging and prostrate, groundcover varieties to columnar varieties up to 3 m tall. Most are well-suited to culinary uses.

Tall varieties include 'Tuscan Blue' syn. 'Erectus', with large leaves, and the delightfully scented 'Portuguese Pink' with pink flowers.

Among the most intensely blue-flowered bush forms are 'Collingwood Ingram' syn. 'Majorca' and 'Benenden Blue', 'Salem', 'Blue Lagoon', 'Severn Sea', 'Corsican Blue', the violet blue-flowered 'Miss Jessup's Upright', 'Suffolk Blue', the excellent 'Herb Cottage' and the strong-growing, superbly fragrant 'Gorizia', from the city of Gorizia in northern Italy.

Pink-flowered bush forms include 'Pink', 'Majorca Pink' and 'Provence Pink', while white-flowered forms include 'Wendy's White' syn. 'Upright White', 'Sissinghurst White' syn. 'Albus' and 'Nancy Howard'.

Semi-prostrate forms ideal for trailing over walls include the glossy-leafed, mid-blue 'Lockwood de Forest', 'Fota Blue', the sky-blue-flowered 'Prostratus', 'Santa Barbara', 'Huntington Carpet' and the beautiful 'Shimmering Stars', with pink buds and blue flowers.

Rosemary
(*Rosmarinus officinalis*)

- **Growing** Rosemary requires full sunshine and excellent drainage. Propagate by tip cuttings taken in early autumn or spring. Bushes respond well to pruning and shaping, and regular light trimming allows good aeration of the foliage and inhibits fungal wilts.
- **Harvesting and storing** In milder climates, you can take clippings of rosemary any time of the year, then air-dry in a well-ventilated place. When completely dry, strip the whole leaves from the stems and store in airtight bottles. Major harvesting should be done before flowering. Gather fresh flowers to use as a garnish on salads and desserts.

Herbal medicine

Rosmarinus officinalis. Parts used: leaves, flowering tops. The medicinal properties of rosemary as a tonic and stimulant to the nerves and circulation make it a popular remedy for combating general fatigue and improving poor circulation. Rosemary also enhances memory and concentration by increasing blood flow to the head. Add a few drops of rosemary essential oil to a vaporiser in the area where you are working or studying.

The essential oil can be applied topically in a diluted form to relieve muscle cramps and arthritic joint pain. It also has a reputation for preventing premature baldness.

For the safe and appropriate medicinal use of rosemary, consult your healthcare professional. Do not use rosemary in greater than culinary quantities if you are pregnant or breastfeeding.

Lest we forget

In Australia and New Zealand, on 25 April, Anzac Day, veterans wear sprigs of rosemary in their lapels to remember and commemorate the fallen. Traditionally a herb of remembrance, rosemary grows wild on the Gallipoli peninsula in Turkey, where Anzac soldiers fought the Turks in World War I.

The basic Hungary water formula uses lavender, rosemary and myrtle, but other herbs can be added.

Hungary water

Until the invention of eau de cologne, this recipe was Europe's favourite fragrance, but it also became popular as a cure-all remedy for everything from dizziness, rheumatism, stomach cramps and headaches to indigestion and lack of appetite. The story of its invention is unclear, but it is thought that, in the 13th century, a hermit gave the recipe to Queen Isabella of Hungary, whose legs were crippled with rheumatism. Daily bathing in this water was said to have restored her legs and also her youthful beauty. Later additions to the formula included thyme, sage, mint and marjoram.

In this Hungary water recipe, a 'handful' is the number of 30-cm lengths of herb stems that can be encircled by the hand.

4.5 litres brandy or clear spirit
1 handful flowering rosemary tops
1 handful lavender
1 handful myrtle

Cut the herbs into 2.5-cm lengths and leave to macerate for a minimum of 2 weeks before filtering.

Around the home

Rosemary is one of the main ingredients in the famous antiseptic Vinegar of the Four Thieves, *page 160*, and can be used in a number of ways around the home.

- Make a simple rosemary disinfectant by simmering a handful of leaves and small stems in water for 30 minutes. Strain and decant into a spray bottle.
- Disinfect and deodorise hairbrushes and combs by soaking them in a solution of 1 cup (250 ml) hot water, 1 tablespoon bicarbonate of soda and 5 drops rosemary essential oil.
- Use dried rosemary in moth-repellent sachets and in pot-pourri.
- Use a rosemary rinse on your dog after washing to deter fleas.
- Wash your pet's bedding, then add a few drops of rosemary essential oil to the final rinse. Or, spritz your pets with rosemary disinfectant as they dry themselves in the sun after a bath.

You can crystallise the flowers of rosemary with egg white and caster sugar for cake decoration (see *page 89*).

Rosemary tea makes a fragrant final rinse for darkening brunette hair.

A herb of goodness

Rosemary has a strong association with the Virgin Mary. It is said that, when the Holy family was fleeing from Herod's soldiers, Mary spread her blue cloak over a white-flowering rosemary bush to dry, but when she removed the cloak, the white flowers had turned blue in her honour. Also associated with ancient magical lore, rosemary was often called 'Elf Leaf', and bunches of it were hung around houses to keep thieves and witches out and to prevent fairies entering and stealing infants.

Cooking

The bruised leaves of rosemary have a cooling pine-like fragrance, with mint and eucalyptus overtones, and the strong taste can overwhelm other flavours if used too generously.

It complements similarly strong flavours such as wine and garlic; starchy foods (bread, scones, potatoes); rich meats such as lamb, pork, duck, goat and game; vegetables such as eggplants, zucchini and brassicas; and is also used in sausages, stuffings, soups and stews. Fresh sprigs are steeped in vinegar or olive oil to flavour them. Rosemary flowers can be added to salads.

The leaves have a rather woody texture, so use them finely chopped. Alternatively, use whole sprigs, or tie leaves in a square of muslin, and remove just before serving. Dried rosemary has a flavour similar to that of fresh, but its very hard texture may not soften, even on long cooking.

Rosemary is popular in Italian cookery. Make a simple and delicious pizza topping with thinly sliced potatoes, crushed garlic and finely chopped fresh rosemary leaves.

Roast leg of lamb with rosemary

6 sprigs fresh rosemary

2 kg bone-in leg of lamb

2 cloves garlic, sliced

2 tablespoons olive oil

1 garlic bulb, halved

1. Preheat oven to 220°C. Cut 2 rosemary sprigs into short lengths. Using a sharp knife cut slits evenly into the lamb; push the cut rosemary and garlic slices into the slits. Rub lamb with oil and season with salt and black pepper.

2. Place the remaining whole rosemary sprigs in roasting pan with the garlic bulb and lamb. Roast for 20 minutes. Reduce oven temperature to 180°C and cook for a further 1–1½ hours or until done to your liking.

3. One hour before the lamb is ready, add your favourite vegetables to the roasting pan, or roast in a separate pan.

4. Transfer lamb to a carving board; cover loosely with foil. Rest for 15 minutes before carving.

SERVES 8

Herb oils

Quality ingredients make great-tasting oils that enhance dips, marinades, sauces and dressings. Other herbs to try include marjoram or oregano, garlic, chervil, coriander, chives or mint.

....

Basil oil

3 tablespoons fresh basil
2 cups (500 ml) olive oil

1 Place basil in medium bowl and cover with 1 cup (250 ml) boiling water. Stand 2 minutes. Drain; pat leaves dry. Process basil and oil in food processor until combined. Alternatively, finely chop basil, add 2 tablespoons oil and mash basil into oil with a fork. Add remaining oil.

2 Leave 2 to 3 days to allow flavours to develop. Strain oil through muslin; pour into clean 500 ml bottle. Store in a cool, dark place. Use in salads.

MAKES 2 CUPS (500 ml)

Rosemary oil

2–3 large sprigs fresh rosemary
3 cloves garlic
3 fresh bay leaves
2 cups (500 ml) olive oil

1 Lightly bruise rosemary, garlic and bay leaves by hitting them with the flat of a knife. Place herbs in clean 500 ml bottle; pour in olive oil.

2 Leave 2 to 3 days to allow flavours to develop. Store in a cool, dark place. Use with pork and lamb.

MAKES 2 CUPS (500 ml)

Lemongrass oil

2–3 fresh lime leaves
1 lemongrass stem
2 cloves garlic
3 slices fresh ginger, each 5 mm thick
2 cups (500 ml) peanut oil

1 Lightly bruise lime leaves, lemongrass, garlic and ginger by hitting them with the flat of a knife. Place herbs in clean 500 ml bottle; pour in oil.

2 Leave 3 to 4 days to allow flavours to develop. Store in a cool, dark place. Use with fish and seafood.

MAKES 2 CUPS (500 ml)

Chilli oil

2 cups (500 ml) olive oil
1–2 whole dried red chillies
20 g dried red chilli flakes
2 extra dried chillies for decoration

1 Place oil, chillies and chilli flakes in a heavy-based saucepan. Warm gently for 3 to 4 minutes; allow to cool.

2 Leave 2 to 3 days to allow flavours to develop. Strain oil through muslin; pour into clean 500 ml bottle. Add the 2 extra whole chillies for decoration. Store in a cool, dark place. Use for stir-fries, in marinades or to drizzle over noodles.

MAKES 2 CUPS (500 ml)

Rosemary oil, Lemongrass oil and Basil oil

Change herbs with the season. The more robust the herb, the better the finished oil.

Sage

There are more than 700 species of salvias, many of them spectacular when in flower, and a number with leaves that release fruit fragrances when brushed.

Latin name *Salvia* sp. Lamiaceae
Parts used Leaves, roots, seeds, flowers

Common sage (*Salvia officinalis*)

🍃 Gardening

Common or garden sage (*S. officinalis*) is one of the best known culinary herbs, but there are also many ornamental species, all with small, lipped flowers in delightful shades, from white to dark purple.

A subshrub native to the Dalmatian Coast, common sage has silver-grey leaves and spikes of attractive lavender, pink or white flowers. It is a pleasantly pungent culinary herb, which also aids digestion.

In addition to the common form of garden sage, there are handsome broad-leaf varieties, such as 'Berggarten', and coloured-leaf forms, such as the purple-leafed 'Purpurea' and the gold- and green-variegated 'Icterina'.

Three–leafed sage (*S. fruticosa*), native to Greece and Turkey, closely resembles garden sage except that most leaves are subtended by a basal pair of leaflets. The dried leaves are often sold as 'garden sage'.

Spanish sage (*S. lavandulifolia*), also known as lavender sage, has narrow leaves and a lavender-and-sage fragrance. Its oil is extracted for toiletries.

Clary sage or muscatel sage (*S. sclarea*), a biennial, is one of the most beautiful sages, with, pebble-textured leaves and tall dense spikes of large pink flowers. The leaves add a muscatel flavour to a diverse range of liqueurs, vermouths and wines, while the essential oil is used in perfumery.

The golden chia (*S. columbariae*), an annual, is native to the southwest of North America. Like chia (*S. hispanica*), which was cultivated as an important staple crop by the Aztecs until colonisation by the Spanish, it produces tiny oily seeds that are gluten-free, very rich in omega-3 fatty acids (alpha-linolenic acid), and high in anti-oxidants, vitamins, minerals and fibre.

The desire of sage is to render man immortal.

From a medieval manuscript

Use the flowers and leaves of pineapple sage (*S. elegans* syn. *S. rutilans*) to garnish salads and desserts and to flavour drinks.

Potted salvias make a pretty display, but are not suited to long-term indoor life. They are easily infested with white fly and scale.

Fragrant-leafed species Some of these species find culinary uses. Pineapple sage (*S. elegans* syn. *S. rutilans*) has slender spikes of red flowers and pineapple-scented leaves used to flavour drinks and garnish desserts.

Others include its variety 'Honey Melon'; fruit salad or peach sage (*S. dorisiana*), with large, lush spikes of rose-pink flowers and fruit-scented leaves.

• Growing With few exceptions, the *Salvia* genus, particularly the grey-leafed species, requires a sunny, well-drained position. Sages are propagated from seed, or by tip cuttings or division for named varieties. Most shrubby salvias respond well to gentle pruning or pinching back, particularly after flowering. Do not heavily fertilise these plants. Pick caterpillars off by hand. Sudden wilting indicates poor drainage and root rot.

• Harvesting and storing Harvest fresh leaves and flowers for culinary use at any time. Dry individual leaves and sprigs before flowering; spread them out in a well-aired place, then store in airtight containers.

Keep feet sweet

Your feet have more sweat glands than any other part of your body, but they're usually trapped inside shoes for most of the day. This astringent herbal foot spray is one way to keep them odour-free.

Make strong sage tea by steeping 2 tablespoons of dried sage in 100 ml boiling water; allow to cool completely. Then add 50 ml of witch hazel and 10 drops of lavender essential oil. Pour into a spray bottle. Refrigerate. Shake well before use. Apply daily. Use within 10 days.

Variegated sage (*S. officinalis* 'Tricolor') makes a striking addition to the herb garden. Younger leaves are pink-edged.

Cooking

Of the many types, which differ widely in flavour, common sage (*S. officinalis*) is the one most often used for cooking. The aroma is highly pungent, while the flavour, which intensifies on drying, is savoury, with camphorous overtones.

Sage goes with starchy, rich and fatty foods such as duck, with poultry and pork (and stuffings for them), red meats, beans, eggplant, tomato-based sauces, casseroles and soups, and also in commercially prepared stuffing mixes and Italian dried mixed herbs. You can also use deep-fried leaves as a garnish.

Best used with a light hand in long-cooked dishes, sage is popular in Italy, less so in France. In the Middle East, it is used in salads. Sage tea is popular in many European countries. In Dalmatia, where sage grows wild, the flowers are used to make honey.

Herbal medicine

Salvia officinalis. Part used: leaves. Sage is an anti-inflammatory and antimicrobial remedy, and is used as a mouthwash and gargle for gum infections, sore throats, tonsillitis and mouth ulcers. It is a popular herb for the treatment of night sweats associated with menopause. Sage also has a beneficial effect on the mind, improving memory, concentration and mood.

For safe and appropriate medicinal use, consult your healthcare professional. Do not use in greater than culinary quantities if you're pregnant or breastfeeding.

Around the home

Sage, like so many herbs, is rich in essential oils, antiviral, antibacterial, deodorising and antifungal, and this is reflected by its old French name, *toute bonne*, or 'all is well'. Use the leaves to make the All-purpose herb vinegar spray (see *page 106*), or simply put a few drops of essential oil on a damp cloth when you're wiping down bathroom and kitchen surfaces.

Sage is also a moth-repellent — use it in dried herb or essential oil form to repel clothes moths and pantry moths. In the garden, plant sage to repel cabbage moth.

Vinegar of the Four Thieves

This herbal vinegar is a strong insect repellent that can be used on your skin as well as on socks and shoes to discourage ticks and mites. It is said to have originated during the time of the Black Plague, when a band of thieves used it to avoid catching the disease. In a glass jar, combine 2 litres apple cider vinegar and 2 tablespoons chopped garlic with 2 tablespoons each of the following herbs: rosemary, rue, sage, lavender, wormwood and peppermint. Steep the mixture in a sunny spot for about 2 weeks, shaking the jar daily. Strain out the herbs, and retain the liquid. Add several cloves of crushed garlic, and seal again. Leave to soak for 3 days. Strain out the garlic fibre and discard. Label the jar and store it in a cool place. Dilute 50:50 with water if spraying it onto your skin and do a patch test before using. Do not use this vinegar if you are pregnant, and do not use on small children.

Pasta with fresh sage, rocket and fetta

400 g tubular pasta shapes, such as casarecce
  (slim rolled lengths), penne or macaroni
50 g pancetta, finely chopped
2 cloves garlic, finely chopped (optional)
2 French shallots, finely chopped
8 fresh sage leaves, shredded
1 can chickpeas, about 400 g, drained
1 can chopped tomatoes, about 400 g
pinch of sugar
black pepper
50 g rocket, stalks removed if preferred
100 g fetta, crumbled

1 Cook pasta in boiling water for 10–12 minutes,
  or according to the packet instructions, until
  al dente. Drain well.

2 Meanwhile, heat a large frying pan over a medium-
  high heat. Add pancetta, garlic, if using, shallots
  and sage. Cook, stirring, for 6–8 minutes, until the
  pancetta is golden brown and the shallots are soft.

3 Add chickpeas, tomatoes and sugar; bring to the
  boil. Reduce heat and simmer for 10 minutes or until
  the sauce has thickened slightly. Season with black
  pepper (no need for salt as fetta is quite salty).

4 Stir in pasta until it is well coated with sauce
  ingredients. Lightly stir in rocket. Sprinkle with
  fetta and serve.

SERVES 4

St John's wort

Traditionally, golden-flowered St John's wort was hung over entrances and cast on midsummer fires as a herb of great protection and purification.

Latin name *Hypericum perforatum* Clusiaceae (Guttiferae)
Part used Flowering tops

Gardening

Hypericum is a very large genus of about 400 species. *H. perforatum* is a hardy, partially woody perennial, an upright growing, unpleasant smelling, clumping plant which can reach 1 m high. Its small, smooth, oval leaves have numerous tiny oil glands, borne in opposite pairs along the stems.

The small golden yellow flowers are borne in large dense cymes in midsummer. The small, seed capsule contains round black seed. The crushed flowers ooze

St John's wort (*Hypericum perforatum*)

a red, blood-like pigment containing hypericin. Do not confuse St John's wort with the many ornamental *Hypericum* varieties grown in gardens.

● **Growing** This plant is easy to grow in a well-drained, moist to fairly dry soil in full sun to light shade. It can be used for ornamental meadows, but is considered a weed toxic to livestock. It is under statutory control in Australia and New Zealand.

Sow seed as soon as it is ripe in autumn (under protection in colder areas), or in the following spring. Germination can take up to 3 months. You can also divide the runners either in autumn or spring. It is a strong grower requiring little tending.

● **Harvesting and storing** Harvest the flowering heads in early summer, when buds commence opening, and dry them.

Weed warning

St John's wort thrives in almost all conditions. Its sticky seed capsules cling to clothing, fur, footwear and even car tyres, spreading the plant along roads and footways and animal tracks. The plant also creeps underground by rhizomes. It crowds out native species, competes with pasture plants and can trigger skin damage if eaten by livestock. Not surprising, then, that it is considered a noxious weed in many countries, including Australia and New Zealand.

🍃 Herbal medicine

Hypericum perforatum. Part used: flowering tops. Traditionally used for treating nerve pain, including neuralgia and sciatica, and to soothe wounds, burns and insect bites, St John's wort continues to be used for these conditions but these days is better known for its use as an antidepressant.

In the 1990s St John's wort was hailed as 'Nature's Prozac', with a number of clinical trials suggesting that the herb was effective against mild to moderate depression, and concluding that it had a similar effectiveness to other antidepressant medication.

Later studies questioned the herb's antidepressant benefits, and noted a number of serious herb-drug interactions, including rising cholesterol levels in people taking certain types of statin drugs while using St John's wort. Although the excitement that surrounded this herb in the 1990s has dimmed, it still offers moderate mood-lifting benefits for some. St John's wort contains two compounds – hypericin and hyperforin – that are known to counter depression, and many preparations using the herb are produced to contain a fixed level of these constituents.

Laboratory studies have also shown that St John's wort possesses pain-relieving properties. The external use of the red oil prepared from the flowers can help relieve sciatica, shingles, cold sores, genital herpes and rheumatic pain. Topically, the oil is also a valuable wound- and burn-healing remedy and can be used on bruises and sprains.

For the safe and appropriate use of St John's wort, consult a healthcare professional. Do not use St John's wort if you are pregnant or breastfeeding.

The red oil of St John's wort is a traditional treatment for cuts and bruises.

Salad burnet

Sir Francis Bacon, the 16th-century English philosopher, suggested growing cucumber-scented salad burnet along paths 'to perfume the air most delightfully'.

....

Latin name *Sanguisorba minor* syn. *Poterium sanguisorba, Pimpinella sanguisorba* Rosaceae
Also known as Burnet bloodwort
Parts used Leaves, roots

🌿 Gardening

Salad burnet (*S. minor*), a dainty, hardy, evergreen perennial to 45 cm, forms a low rosette of ferny leaves. The tiny green, wind-pollinated flowers with deep red anthers are borne in dense heads on slender stems.

Salad burnet (*Sanguisorba minor*)

Herb cocktail

The cucumber taste of salad burnet makes it an excellent accompaniment to alcoholic drinks; according to the Elizabethan herbal writer Gerard, the plants 'make the heart merry and glad'. For a refreshing cocktail, bruise 6 sprays of salad burnet with a rolling pin or with a mortar and pestle, then place in a large jug containing 750 ml sweet white wine, 500 ml sherry and 1 thinly sliced lemon. Mix well; allow to infuse for at least 2 hours. Sweeten to taste. Add 1 litre of soda water and serve over crushed ice.

• **Position** These plants prefer full sun to partial shade, and a well-drained, moist soil that contains compost. Sow seed in either spring or autumn. Plants that are allowed to flower will self-seed, producing particularly healthy plants.
• **Harvesting and storing** Harvest leaves for medicinal use before flowering. For fresh use, harvest leaves as required. Lift roots in autumn for drying.

🌿 Herbal medicine

Sanguisorba officinalis syn. *Poterium officinalis*. Parts used: leaves, roots. Greater burnet has a very long tradition of use in Western and Chinese medicine. The plant is astringent due to the presence of some unusual tanins, together with gums and glycosides. It is used externally in treating minor burns and scalds, sores and skin infections, and to staunch bleeding.

🌿 Cooking

Salad burnet is an ingredient in several sauces, including ravigote, which is used in French cooking and goes well with cold roast chicken or seafood. Add the young leaves of salad burnet to salads, chilled summer soups and to soft cheeses. Also use as a garnish or infused in vinegar. This herb does not dry well, but the leaves can be frozen in ice-cube trays.

Savory

Satureja is reputed to have been the source of the mythical satyrs' enormous sexual stamina. They are said to have worn crowns of the aromatic herbs.

Summer savory
(*Satureja hortensis*)

Latin name *Satureja* sp. Lamiaceae
Part used Leaves

Gardening

Summer savory (*S. hortensis*), an annual growing to 45 cm, has slender dark green leaves, pink flowers and an aroma of thyme and oregano. Winter savory (*S. montana*) is a perennial subshrub with dark green, narrow-leafed foliage and white flowers. Creeping savory (*S. montana* subsp. *montana* var. *prostata*) is semi-prostrate, very ornamental and resembles white heather when in flower.

Thyme-leafed savory or za'atar rumi or savory of Crete or pink savory (*S. thymbra*) is a low-growing, stiffly branched perennial with whorls of small greyish leaves that have an intense oregano and thyme fragrance and flavour.

- **Growing** All species require full sun and a well-drained soil. In cold areas, give plants winter protection. Sow seed shallowly in spring. Perennial species are also propagated by cuttings in spring and early autumn.
- **Harvesting and storing** You can cut down whole plants of *S. hortensis* before flowering and dry them. Harvest the leaves of other species fresh as required, and dry or freeze them in sealed containers.

Cooking

Both summer and winter savory have a similar aroma — fragrant, with a hint of thyme, and a peppery taste, although the flavour of winter savory is stronger and more pungent. The flavour is better before the plant flowers. Savory retains its flavour when dried; in this form it is preferred for cooking.

Savory goes well with lentils and peas, slow-cooked soups, stews, meatloaf and egg dishes. Use it in coatings for delicate meats, such as veal, and for fish. Add to sauces, pâtés and homemade sausages. It is a key herb in Herbes de Provence (see below). Use summer savory in marinades, especially for olives. In Croatian cooking, a lemon-scented variety is used with seafood.

Herbes de Provence

Use this classic herb mix to season vegetables, chicken and red meat.

4 tablespoons dried rosemary leaves
3 tablespoons dried sweet marjoram leaves
2 tablespoons dried thyme leaves
3 tablespoons dried savory leaves
2 tablespoons dried lavender flowers
1 teaspoon dried sage leaves

1 Combine the dried herbs. Place in an airtight container.

2 Store in a cool, dark place for up to 4 months. If using the mix with fish, add a pinch of fennel seeds.

Scented geranium

Scented geraniums are the great mimics of the plant world. At the slightest touch they release intense true-to-name fragrances, from cloves and ripe apples to red roses.

....

Latin name *Pelargonium* sp. Geraniaceae
Parts used Leaves, roots, flowers

Pelargonium quercifolium 'Fair Ellen'

Gardening

The species used to create the scented geraniums originated in the Cape of Good Hope area in South Africa. They were introduced into England as a curiosity in the 1630s, but by the 1840s the French realised their potential as an essential oil source. Steam distillation of rose geranium (*P. graveolens*) yields an essential oil with a rose fragrance that is used in perfumes and toiletries.

The scented geraniums are soft to semi-hard wooded shrubs or subshrubs with a very wide range of leaf shapes. *P. graveolens* is an upright multi-stemmed small shrub to 90 cm, with bright green, much indented leaves that create a lacy shape. The small flowers are mid-pink rouged with bright ruby on the upper petals. Other rose-scented species distilled for oil are *P. capitatum* and its variety 'Attar of Roses', together with *P. radens*.

Scented geraniums became great favourites with 19th-century gardeners in Europe, as they proved adaptable to cultivation in conservatories and on sunny parlour windowsills during the winter months

• **Growing** Scented geraniums are drought-resistant, and, where space is limited, a collection can be kept in well-drained pots in a sunny position. Grow from 10-cm cuttings taken in late summer. Water thoroughly when the upper soil dries out.

• **Harvesting and storing** Harvest and dry leaves at any time for use in pot-pourri (see *page 97*) and herbal sleep pillows (see *page 111*). Harvesting for distillation occurs around midsummer.

Rose geranium (*Pelargonium graveolens*)

Peppermint geranium leaves make an instant poultice for sprains and bruises.

Natural beauty

Rose geranium (*Pelargonium graveolens*) is the classic beauty pick-me-up. The toning effect of its essential oil revives tired skin and the fresh, pungent smell revives body and mind. Its toning and balancing properties leave hair and scalp clean and fresh.

Rose geranium essential oil is much valued in aromatherapy, and is used in massage oils to relieve tension and soothe the symptoms of dermatitis and eczema. The oil is a mild anti-irritant, making it helpful for any inflammation, including minor wounds and insect bites. It also helps control stress-triggered oil production, which can result in pimple breakouts; in the early 1900s, it enjoyed a rather controversial success as a remedy for this condition in Europe.

Around the home

Rose geranium oil can be used as a tick repellent for dogs, and is considered both mosquito- and lice-repellent. The oil of apple geranium (*P. odoratissimum*) is astringent and antiseptic, and repels insects.

Fabric softener

This simple treatment will leave fabrics soft and fluffy without the cloying scent of artificial perfumes.

1 cup (250 ml) white distilled vinegar
1 cup (250 g) bicarbonate of soda
2 cups (500 ml) water
10 drops rose geranium, lavender
   or lemon essential oil or eucalyptus oil
   (or a combination of your favourite oils)

1 Combine ingredients slowly and carefully over the sink, because the mixture will fizz. Pour into a plastic bottle and replace the lid.

2 Add ¼ cup (60 ml) to the final rinse or place it in the fabric softener dispenser of your washing machine.

Cooking with scented geraniums

Scented geraniums, with their attractive leaves in a wide range of heavenly scents, are a culinary treat. Try using them in the following ways.

☐ Add dried leaves of rose or lemon varieties to the tea caddy.

☐ Finely chop fresh leaves. Infuse in warmed liquid such as cream or milk. Strain, and use liquid to make ice-creams, sweet custards and sauces for desserts.

☐ Infuse red wine vinegar with rose geranium and fresh raspberries. Strain after a week for a summer salad vinegar.

☐ Place a cake still warm from the oven on top of leaves to absorb the fragrance. Try rose geranium with vanilla pound cake or peppermint geranium with a chocolate sponge. Remove the leaves when the cake has cooled.

☐ Line jelly moulds with leaves and pour a jelly on top to set.

Sorrel

Sorrel is easily grown, and the fresh lemony flavour of its young leaves is very versatile in dishes such as salads, soups and frittatas. Sorrel is high in vitamin A.

....

Latin name *Rumex acetosa, R. scutatus, R. acetosella* Polygonaceae
Parts used Leaves (sorrel); roots (yellow dock)

French sorrel (*Rumex scutatus*)

🌿 Gardening

Three species of sorrel are grown for culinary purposes — broad leaf, garden or sheep's sorrel, or sour grass (*R. acetosa*); French or buckler-leaf sorrel (*R. scutatus*); and sheep's sorrel (*R. acetosella*).

Broad leaf sorrel is a perennial forming a basal rosette of leaves up to 15 cm long. In early summer the slender flowering stems, to about 1.2 m, produce spikes of tiny reddish flowers. 'Blond de Lyon', a variety of *R. acetosa* with large succulent leaves, is used for classic sorrel soup and to produce blue and green dyes.

French sorrel has smaller leaves, tiny green flowers and grows to about 30 cm.

• **Growing** Sorrel requires a rich, moist soil and a sunny to partly shaded position. Sow seed in situ when the soil has warmed in spring, or start it indoors and transplant it. Seeds germinate within 14 days. Regularly trim plants of culinary sorrels to keep up the supply of fresh, tender young leaves. Remove the flowering heads whenever they appear.

• **Harvesting and storing** Pick sorrel fresh throughout the growing

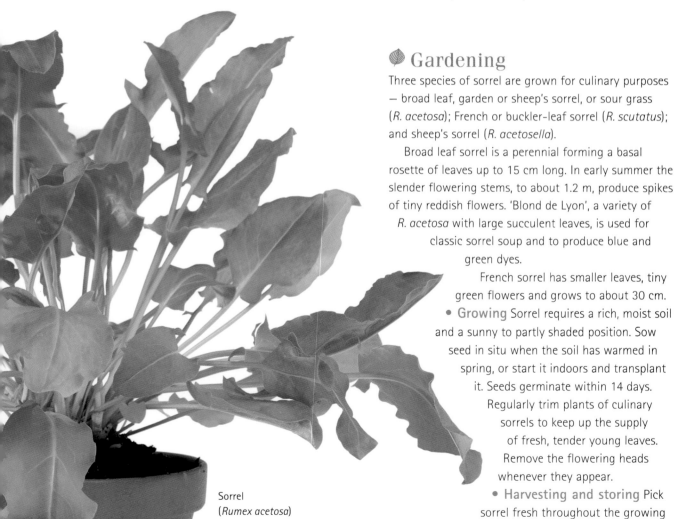

Sorrel
(*Rumex acetosa*)

season. It does not dry well but, like spinach, it can be frozen. Lift the roots in autumn and dry them for herbal preparations.

Cooking

This spinach-like leaf is quite delicious if picked in spring, when young and tender. Cook it briefly to retain the flavour; do not use aluminium or iron pots or utensils, as they will make sorrel go black and cause a disagreeable metallic taste. If using raw, select the young, tender leaves. A purée of cooked sorrel is a good accompaniment to fish, eggs, pork and veal. Sorrel's acidity also acts as a meat tenderiser.

French sorrel is best if picked when young.

Sorrels and docks

Sheep's sorrel (*Rumex acetosella*) and other members of the sorrel family have been associated with a marked diuretic effect, and were often taken as a traditional spring tonic. A juice or infusion of fresh leaves was used to reduce fevers.

Sheep's sorrel is commonly found as an ingredient in a herbal formula called Essiac Tea, said to be based on a traditional Native American remedy. While there's no scientific evidence to confirm its immune-stimulating properties, the tea has been used since the 1920s by cancer patients and more recently by those with HIV and diabetes.

Yellow dock (*Rumex crispus*) is a relative of the sorrels. It is used for chronic skin conditions and for arthritic complaints. Herbalists believe that these conditions are related to a toxin build-up in the body; yellow dock root may alleviate them by enhancing the detoxifying capacity of the liver as well as encouraging more efficient removal of toxins as a result of a gentle laxative action. Considered weedy, the plant is under statutory control in Australia.

Sweet cicely

This delightfully ornamental herb has leaves with a sugary anise scent. The cooked young roots were once considered beneficial for those who were 'dull and without courage'.

Latin name *Myrrhis odorata* Apiaceae
Also known as English myrrh
Parts used Young leaves and stalks, young roots

Sweet cicely (*Myrrhis odorata*)

Gardening

Native to cool, moist mountainous areas of Europe, sweet cicely is the lone species in its genus. It is a fully hardy perennial, forming a clump of delicate, fern-like and very sweet-tasting leaves. The large, handsome heads of white flowers are followed by slender, 2.5-cm seeds, which are technically fruits. They are aromatic and deliciously nutty when eaten raw and green. Both the leaves and green fruits are very high in anethole, which gives them their sweet anise scent. Mature seeds are a shiny dark brown.

Sweet cicely, American style

Osmorhiza longistylis, a native North American species of Apiaceae, also known as sweet cicely (or aniseroot, licoriceroot or longstyle sweetroot), is a perennial with small, white umbelliferous inflorescences and coarse, rather celery-like leaves. It is found in rich woodland in eastern North America. The sweet-tasting root, with its strong anise scent, was used by Native Americans as a digestive and antiseptic.

• **Growing** Sweet cicely requires a humus-rich moist soil, a cool climate and a shady location. Allow the seed to fall around the parent plants, where they will germinate in spring. Remove flowering stalks to prolong leaf production.
• **Harvesting and storing** Harvest young leaves for fresh use. They retain little fragrance after drying. Pickle the unripe seeds, and clean and store the young roots in brandy.

Cooking

Boil the roots as a vegetable; they can also be candied like angelica and used as a decoration for desserts. Use the crisp, celery-tasting stems in salads.

The leaves of sweet cicely have a warm, anise aroma and a pleasantly sweet taste. Use them fresh in salads or add them when cooking sharp fruits such as gooseberries and rhubarb, as their natural sweetness will counteract the tartness. They are a safe sweetener for diabetics. The green seeds can be used for the same purpose. The herb is an ingredient in Chartreuse liqueur, and is also included in Scandinavian aquavit, used as a digestive and an aperitif.

Sweet cicely leaves add a lovely flavour to cream, yogurt, rice pudding, fruit and wine cups, soups, stews and dressings. Use leaves in omelettes and soups, too. They also make a very pretty garnish.

Sweet myrtle

Myrtle was sacred to Venus in ancient times, and groves of fragrant myrtles were grown around her temples. Brides still tuck sprigs of myrtle into their bouquets.

Sweet myrtle (*Myrtus communis*)

Latin name *Myrtus communis* Myrtaceae
Also known as Greek myrtle
Parts used Leaves, buds, flowers, fruits

Gardening

Sweet myrtle is native to the southeastern Mediterranean. The sweetly spicy essential oil, also known as *eau d'anges* (angel's water), is used in perfumery and for medicinal purposes. The plant varies from a shrub to a small tree with oval, shiny, fragrant green leaves and small white flowers with a central 'powder puff' of stamens.

• **Growing** Sweet myrtle requires sunshine and good drainage. You can propagate myrtle by seed, although the resulting plants can be quite variable.

• **Harvesting and storing** You can air-dry the buds, flowers, fruits and leaves.

Cooking

Although of limited culinary use, the leaves, flower buds and fruits of sweet myrtle feature in Mediterranean cooking, especially Corsican and Sardinian recipes, to flavour pork, lamb and small game birds. They are also used in sauces and some liqueurs.

The berries have a mild juniper flavour, and both the dried flowers and dried fruits are ground into a spice that has the same flavour. The infused oil is used in teas, salad dressings, fish and chicken dishes, desserts and bakery items.

Lay myrtle sprigs over barbecued or roast meats towards the end of cooking to add a spicy flavour.

Other myrtles

Lemon myrtle (*Backhousia citriodora*), cinnamon myrtle (*B. myrtifolia*) and anise or aniseed myrtle (*Syzygium anisatum*) are rainforest trees from eastern Australia that are rapidly gaining prominence for their culinary and perfumery uses; they are now plantation grown. Lemon myrtle is a broad-leafed evergreen tree with panicles of small, scented white flowers. The leaves have an intensely fresh lemon fragrance, and the essential oil is typically very high in citral. Anise or aniseed myrtle is used in teas and also as a culinary flavouring. Cinnamon myrtle or carrol forms a shrub–tree with spicy cinnamon-scented ovate leaves that can be used in cooking. Bog myrtle or sweet gale (*Myrica gale*) of the family Myricaeae has sweetly resinous leaves that repel insects. They are used in perfumery, as a condiment, and also in treating skin problems.

Experiment with unusual containers, such as wicker baskets and old colanders.

Sweet violet

The sweet fragrance of violets is often detected on early spring breezes long before the flowers are seen, leading to sayings such as 'shy violet' and 'modest as a violet'.

Latin name *Viola odorata* Violaceae
Parts used Leaves, flowers

Sweet violet (*Viola odorata*)

 Gardening

Sweet violets hold a proud place in history, associating freely with poets and emperors. They were sold in the markets of ancient Greece, are mentioned frequently in the writings of Homer and Virgil and were the favourite flowers of Napoléon and Josephine.

Of the 250 or so species of *Viola*, two are used medicinally: *V. odorata* (sweet violet) and *V. tricolor* (see Heartsease, *page 88*). There are single, semi-double and fully double forms of *V. odorata* occurring naturally in a number of different colours.

Among recommended garden varieties of sweet violets are 'Victoria', which is the foundation of the French Riviera industry; 'Princess of Wales' (grown commercially in Australia); sky-blue 'John Raddenbury'; red-purple 'Admiral Avellan'; pink 'Rosina'; the richly coloured 'Queen of Burgundy'; white 'Alba'; apricot-coloured 'Crépuscule'; and the large purple- and white-striped 'King of the Doubles'.

The very double Parma violets have shiny heart-shaped leaves and profuse, large, intensely fragrant flowers that resemble rosebuds.

● **Growing** Sweet violets thrive in a well-composted, moist soil. Flowering is reduced in shaded locations, so a position under deciduous trees is ideal. Mulching ensures good summer growth. Propagate plants by runners formed in autumn. Remove old plants when they become woody. Apply a liquid seaweed fertiliser once or twice annually; overfeeding encourages foliage rather than flowers.

● **Harvesting and storing** Gather flowers and leaves fresh when in season.

Napoléon and Josephine

In the 19th century, when violets were very fashionable, entire districts were devoted to their production. Victorian women pinned sweet-scented corsages to their gowns, and the fragrance was captured in many products, from perfumes to toiletries, prepared from the essential oil, which is distilled from the leaves. Josephine, wife of the French emperor Napoléon, loved the scent of violets. After his death, sweet violets and a lock of her hair were found in a locket he had kept.

🍃 Herbal medicine

Viola odorata. Parts used: leaves, flowers. The medicinal properties of sweet violet are very similar to those attributed to its relative, heartsease (*V. tricolor*). Sweet violet is used for skin conditions such as eczema and psoriasis as well as catarrhal conditions of the respiratory tract, where it can help remove mucus from the lungs. In traditional herbal practice, sweet violet has a reputation as an adjunctive remedy in the treatment of certain types of cancer.

For the safe and appropriate use of sweet violet, consult your healthcare professional. Do not use sweet violet if you are pregnant or breastfeeding.

Forgiveness is the fragrance that violet sheds on the heel that has crushed it.

Mark Twain
American writer 1835–1910

Cool and pretty

To add a splash of colour to summer drinks, freeze sweet violet and heartsease flowers in water in ice-cube trays and then pop a few cubes into a jug of lemonade.

🍃 Cooking

The flowers of sweet violet are edible and, from the time of the ancient Romans, who used the fragrant blooms to sweeten their wine, have a long history of culinary use. In Victorian times, fresh flowers were used to create herbal jellies, syrups, pastilles, liqueurs and chocolates.

You can use freshly picked flowers to garnish and add flavour to desserts and fruit salads. Like heartsease, sweet violets can be crystallised for cake decoration (see *page 89*).

The flowers and young leaves can be scattered through salads and the flowers can be made into tea or steeped in vinegar to add both flavour and a delicate mauve tint.

Sweet violets grow well in dappled shade beneath deciduous trees.

Sweet woodruff

Sweet woodruff and its relatives, ladies' bedstraw, madder and cleavers, have all been used since medieval times, both as flavourings and as strewing herbs.

Sweet woodruff (*Galium odoratum*)

Latin name *Galium odoratum* syn. *Asperula odorata* Rubiaceae
Parts used Leaves (*G. odoratum*, *G. verum*), flowers (*G. odoratum*), roots (*Rubia tinctorium*), whole plant (*G. aparine*)

🌿 Gardening

Sweet woodruff (*G. odoratum*) is a perennial growing to about 23 cm. It has whorls of shiny leaves and bears loose clusters of starry white flowers.
Ladies' bedstraw (*G. verum*), also known as yellow bedstraw and Our Lady's bedstraw, resembles a slender form of sweet woodruff. 'Bedstraw' refers to the plant's former use as mattress stuffing.
Cleavers or goosegrass (*G. aparine*), an annual resembling a coarse version of sweet woodruff, has white flowers and stems and leaves that are covered with hooked bristles. Cleavers has been used as a pot herb, and its seed roasted as a good coffee substitute.
Madder (*Rubia tinctorium*), a scrambling perennial with starry yellow flowers, resembles a larger and coarser version of sweet woodruff. The roots can reach 1 m long and are the source of a valuable pigment, red madder, which is used to make fabric dye, inks and paints.
• **Growing** Sweet woodruff and its relatives all prefer a moist, compost-enriched soil. Woodruff and cleavers prefer a partly shaded position, while bedstraw requires full sun. Grow sweet woodruff, ladies' bedstraw and madder by seed or by division; grow cleavers by seed.

• **Harvesting and storing** Harvest sweet woodruff and bedstraw, then air-dry as required. Once dried, sweet woodruff develops a pleasing scent of fresh-mown hay. When madder roots are 2 years old, strip them of bark and dry them. They are used to make dye.

Traditional uses

Woodruff was once used as a strewing herb because it produces a fresh hay-like scent as it dries. Traditionally, it was used as a flavouring for jellies, jams and ice-creams as well as beer and sausages in Germany, where it is now replaced with synthetic flavourings and aromas. Woodruff is still in use as a flavouring for tobacco.

Ladies' bedstraw (right) has long been used to curdle milk for making cheeses, especially vegetarian types, while its roots were used to dye tartans in Scotland until 1695, when the erosion of native grasslands resulted in the practice being banned.

Tansy

A bitter herb included in liqueurs, in medieval times tansy was eaten in dishes as a penance at Eastertide. It was also used as a remedy for intestinal worms.

....

Latin name *Tanacetum vulgare* syn.
Chrysanthemum vulgare Asteraceae
Also known as Golden buttons
Parts used Aerial parts

🌿 Gardening

A very hardy rhizomatous perennial herb, tansy grows to about 1.2 m. Its leaves typically have a camphor scent. It bears flat-topped clusters of golden button flowers that dry well.

Bible leaf

Costmary, so named because it was dedicated to the Virgin Mary, once also had the common name of bible leaf, in reference to its use as a Bible bookmark – its mint-like scent was perfect for reviving the faint-hearted during long Sunday sermons. The word *tanacetum* is from *athanasia*, Greek for 'immortality', reflecting the fact that the plant stays in flower for a long period. In ancient Greece, corpses were packed with tansy leaves to preserve them and ward off insects until burial took place.

Crisp-leafed or fern-leafed or curly tansy is a more compact ornamental form with ferny leaves. Costmary or alecost or bible leaf (*T. balsamita*) is a rhizomatous perennial with clusters of white daisy flowers and silvery green, mint-scented leaves. Camphor plant (*T. balsamita* subsp. *tomentosum*) has camphor-scented foliage and is used in moth-repellent herb mixtures.

• **Growing** Tansy prefers a well-drained, sunny position. Propagate by seed, root division in spring or semi-ripe tip cuttings in summer. It can become invasive, so in garden beds take care to keep the rhizomes under control.

• **Harvesting and storing** Harvest tansy foliage during flowering for drying or oil extraction. Harvest the leaves of costmary and camphor plant as required.

🌿 Around the home

A natural insect repellent, tansy can be grown outside in pots around outdoor entertaining areas to deter flies and mosquitoes.

Indoors, use dried tansy to deter ants, clothes moths or fleas in your pet's bedding. A strong tansy tea can be spritzed over the carpet to keep flea populations under control, but do not spray it directly onto your pet or its bedding. Also, do not use it if you are pregnant or breastfeeding.

Tansy (*Tanacetum vulgare*)

Herbs love growing in pots. Give them the right position and good care and they will flourish.

Tarragon

Dracunculus is Latin for 'little dragon', and once tarragon was reputed to cure the bites of not only diminutive dragons but of all serpents and other venomous creatures.

....

Latin name *Artemisia dracunculus*, *A. dracunculoides* Asteraceae
Part used Leaves

🍃 Gardening

French tarragon (*A. dracunculus*) is a selected form of exceptional flavour. It rarely sets seed, especially in cool climates. Its slender linear leaves are warmly aromatic, with a complex fragrance and taste that blends sweet anise, basil and resinous undertones.

Russian tarragon (*A. dracunculoides*) regularly flowers and sets viable seeds. It often improves in flavour the longer it is grown, but seed-grown Russian tarragon has an earthy balsamic scent.

• **Position** French tarragon is cold-hardy and drought-resistant, and can grow in high summer temperatures. It is, however, very susceptible to high humidity and easily infected with fungal diseases. Avoid overhead watering. Propagate French tarragon by tip cuttings in spring and early autumn, or by root division.

• **Harvesting and storing** Harvest foliage until mid-autumn.

Tarragon's unique and piquant flavour is indispensable to the classic cuisine of France.

🍃 Herbal medicine

Artemisia dracunculus, A. dracunculoides. Part used: leaves. These days, tarragon is more likely to be used for culinary than therapeutic purposes. Tarragon contains an essential oil component that is reputed to have similar properties to that of anise, which is often used to treat digestive symptoms. Russian tarragon has been used for stimulating the appetite.

In some countries, tarragon is traditionally used to treat the symptoms of diabetes; recent scientific research appears to support this. Preliminary studies in diabetic animals found that an alcoholic extract of French tarragon lowered the levels of both insulin and glucose in the blood.

For the safe and appropriate medicinal use of tarragon, consult your healthcare professional. Do not use tarragon in greater than culinary quantities if you are pregnant or breastfeeding.

🍃 Cooking

French tarragon's flavour diffuses rapidly through cooked dishes, so use it carefully. Use it fresh with fish and shellfish, turkey, chicken, game, veal and egg dishes. Use chopped leaves in salad dressings, *fines herbes* (see page 40), mustard, ravigote and béchamel sauces, béarnaise sauce, sauce verte and in mayonnaise.

French tarragon
(*Artemisia dracunculus*)

Chicken and vegetable casserole

2 tablespoons olive oil

350 g skinless chicken breasts, cut into small chunks

1 small onion, chopped

250 g button mushrooms

grated zest of 1 lemon

1 fresh bay leaf

2 large sprigs fresh thyme, or ½ teaspoon dried thyme

3 large sprigs fresh tarragon, or ½ teaspoon dried
   tarragon (optional)

150 ml dry sherry

250 g baby carrots, scrubbed

250 g broccoli florets

1 tablespoon cornflour

3 tablespoons chopped fresh flat-leaf parsley

1 Heat oil in a large saucepan, or a deep frying
   pan with a lid. Brown chicken over high heat for
   3 minutes, stirring. Reduce heat to medium.

2 Add onion, mushrooms, lemon zest, bay leaf, thyme
   and tarragon, if using. Sauté for 4 minutes, or until
   vegetables start to soften.

3 Pour in the sherry and 300 ml water. Add carrots,
   season with salt and black pepper and bring to the
   boil. Reduce heat, cover and simmer for 5 minutes.

4 Stir in broccoli. Bring the liquid to a steady simmer.
   Cover and cook for a further 5 minutes, until chicken
   is tender and vegetables are just cooked. Discard bay
   leaf and herb sprigs.

5 Blend cornflour with 2 tablespoons cold water;
   stir into casserole. Simmer for 2 minutes, stirring
   constantly, until the sauce has thickened and is
   smooth. Stir in the parsley and serve.

SERVES 4

Tea

Tea has been the favoured beverage of China for 3000 years. Green tea has been shown to be rich in anti-oxidants and has a number of uses in traditional medicine.

Latin name *Camellia sinensis* syn. *Thea sinensis*
Theaceae
Parts used Leaf tips, leaves, seeds

Gardening

There are some 350 varieties of *Camellia sinensis*, and they vary considerably in form. The smooth, leathery leaves are oval, pointed and faintly scented. The small white flowers are single, with a boss of gold stamens, and are borne in the leaf axils.

Tea contains polyphenol anti-oxidants, the levels being higher in green tea, which has undergone minimal oxidation. An essential oil is distilled from the mature leaves, which is used both in perfumery and as a commercial flavouring. The seeds are pressed for a fixed oil that is processed to remove saponins. Other species that are used for oil production include *C. crapnelliana*, *C. oleifera*, *C. octapetala* and *C. sasanqua*.

- **Growing** *Camellia sinensis* is frost-hardy and requires full sun to partial shade, and a rich, moist, but well-drained soil.
- **Harvesting and storing** Harvest leaf tips for tea once bushes are 3 years old.

Herbal medicine

Camellia sinensis. Part used: leaves. Leaves picked from the tea plant are subjected to various processing methods to produce green, black, white and oolong varieties of tea: for instance, leaves are fermented and dried for black tea, but steamed and dried for green tea.

Each type of tea contains different levels of important compounds, known as polyphenols, which are primarily responsible for the plant's medicinal properties. Green tea contains the highest levels of polyphenols and is regarded as having the greatest therapeutic activity of all these teas.

Green tea polyphenols possess a potent anti-oxidant capacity that is far greater than that of vitamin C or E, and which may help in the prevention and treatment of numerous chronic diseases of our time. Studies of large populations of regular green tea drinkers report

Tea (*Camellia sinensis*)

Hand harvesting of *Camellia sinensis* leaves for tea, one of the world's most popular beverages.

lower rates of some cancers and reduced risk of cardio-vascular disease. Green tea also has a protective effect against sunburn when applied topically (see below).

Studies also suggest a potential role for green tea as a weight-loss agent in the treatment of diabetes as a result of a blood glucose-lowering effect in addition to its anti-oxidant properties.

For the safe and appropriate medicinal use of green tea, consult your healthcare professional. Do not use green tea in greater than culinary quantities if you are pregnant or breastfeeding. Caffeine intake should be monitored during these times.

Golden camellia tea is prepared from a rare 'living fossil' species found in China.

Sunburn body spray

Use this remedy to ease the pain of sunburn and speed healing. Green tea contains powerful polyphenols that help to protect skin and slow inflammation triggered by sun exposure. Feverfew reduces redness and lavender is healing.

4 teaspoons green tea
2 teaspoons dried feverfew
½ cup (125 ml) boiling water
¼ cup (60 ml) rosewater
10 drops lavender essential oil

1 Place tea and feverfew in a pot and pour on boiling water. Cover the pot and steep for 15 minutes, then strain and refrigerate.

2 Stir in rosewater and oil. Pour into a spray bottle.

3 To use, shake and lightly mist over skin. Store in the refrigerator. Use the spray within 10 days.

Tea tree

In the 18th century, Aboriginal Australians taught James Cook and his crew how to make poultices of the crushed leaves of tea tree to treat cuts and skin infections.

. . . .

Latin name *Melaleuca* sp. Myrtaceae
Parts used Leaves, branches

🍃 Gardening

'Tea tree' is a misnomer, as that term also applies to *Leptospermum* species, while *Melaleuca* species are actually paperbarks. This has caused confusion and the widely held belief that the 'tea' trialled by the Cook expedition as a cure for scurvy was prepared from *Melaleuca*, which is not recommended.

Tea tree (*M. alternifolia*) is plantation-grown in Australia for high quality essential oil. The species grows to about 7 m and occurs naturally on the warm east coast of Australia, where it is often associated with swampy conditions.

M. leucadendron, a tall species, is the source of cajeput oil. Both *M. viridiflora* and *M. quinquenervia* are sources of niaouli oil, used in perfumery and as an antiseptic. All four species have whitish, layered, papery bark, stiff pointed narrow linear (*M. alternifolia*) or oval smooth leaves, and profuse, intensely honey-scented bottlebrush inflorescences, which are white, except in *M. viridiflora* where they are greenish white or, rarely, pink to red. Trees may literally drip nectar.

- **Growing** The species of *Melaleuca* described require an acid, very moist soil, full sun and warm conditions. All species can be grown by seed, but trees with desirable chemotypes are raised by seed from selected trees or by cuttings. Irrigation is important.
- **Harvesting and storing** Trees are cut for foliage, which is water- or steam-distilled and then cured for 6 weeks.

In the Second World War, Australian soldiers in the tropics used tea-tree oil to treat infections, wounds and tinea.

🍃 Herbal medicine

Melaleuca alternifolia. Parts used: essential oil from leaves and branches. The essential oil of the tea-tree plant was popular with colonial Australians for its antiseptic properties. Scientific research later confirmed that it possesses potent antimicrobial actions against many common bacterial, viral and fungal disease-causing organisms.

These days, tea-tree essential oil continues to be used extensively for its topical antiseptic actions. It is used to treat acne, gum infections and fungal infections of the feet. Use it, diluted, to cleanse wounds at risk of

Tea tree (*Melaleuca alternifolia*)

infection. You can also add it to shampoo to help treat head lice.

Tea-tree oil should not be used internally. Do not use tea-tree oil if you are pregnant or breastfeeding.

Around the home

Tea-tree oil is powerfully antiseptic, with antimicrobial and antibacterial properties.

- Wipe down surfaces with a disinfectant solution – mix tea-tree oil with either water or vinegar.
- Disinfect a shower and remove mould by mixing ¼ cup (60 g) borax, 2 cups very hot water and ¼ teaspoon tea-tree oil. Shake in a spray bottle until borax dissolves. Spray on surfaces, leave overnight, then rinse.
- Deodorise and disinfect garbage bins — wipe them out with a solution of ½ teaspoon tea-tree oil and a little detergent in hot water.

To help repel fleas, spritz your dog with a mixture of 4 drops of tea-tree oil, 4 drops of lavender essential oil and 1 cup of water.

New Zealand tea tree

The essential oil of the New Zealand tea tree or manuka (*Leptospermum scoparium*) is strongly antimicrobial and can be diluted and used to disinfect wounds. A particularly important remedy is honey from bees that graze on manuka. Manuka honey contains a compound called Unique Manuka Factor (UMF), which super-charges its ability to heal infections. Extensive research at the University of Waikato in New Zealand has demonstrated that high-UMF honey disinfects wounds and also encourages them to heal, making it an ideal dressing for leg ulcers and other slow-healing skin infections. High-UMF honey is labelled as 'active manuka' honey. Other manuka honeys without the 'active' label (or a UMF rating of at least 10) are not likely to be as potent.

Thyme

There are an astonishing number of thyme species with a wide variety of fragrances, flavours and uses, from culinary and medicinal to mystical and magical.

....

Latin name *Thymus* sp. Lamiaceae
Part used Leaves

🍃 Gardening

There are some 350 species of thyme. They share much in common, most being sun-loving, perennial woody subshrubs or creeping woody plants with a neat habit that are high in fragrant essential oils.

Garden or common thyme (*T. vulgaris*) is the principal culinary thyme. The leaves of all forms are tiny, narrow, elliptic, grey-green and aromatic. The tiny white or occasionally lavender flowers are borne terminally in many-layered whorls.

Selected forms include 'Silver Posie', with soft green and white variegated foliage; 'German Winter', a very hardy spreading form; 'Provence', a selected high-quality culinary variety from France; a hybrid called 'Fragrantissimus', or orange thyme, with very fine, erect,

Grow common thyme (*Thymus vulgaris*) in pots or as a border plant in the garden.

thyme- and citrus-scented grey foliage; and 'Erectus', with strong vertical growth.

Caraway or seedcake thyme (*T. herba-barona*) is a wiry carpeting thyme with a delicious caraway scent and lavender flowers. The neat foliage is deep green and the loose flower heads are mauve. Varieties include 'Lemon Caraway' and 'Nutmeg'.

Conehead thyme (*T. capitatus* syn. *Coridothymus capitatus*) is another very popular cooking thyme. It is an intensely scented, compact spreading subshrub with distinctive terminal conical clusters of attractive, deep pink flowers.

Spanish thyme (*T. mastichina*) forms a neat grey, upright subshrub. The scent is predominantly of common thyme with an element of eucalyptus leaf. This thyme is excellent for barbecues.

Lemon thyme (*T. x citriodorus*) has neat, bushy, fresh green-leafed plants that are redolent of lemon and thyme, making them ideal for fish and chicken dishes. The plants have

Common thyme (*Thymus vulgaris*)

'Bush BBQ' thyme is very aromatic, perfect for adding flavour to barbecued meat.

Thymus vulgaris 'Silver Posie' bears pink-purple flowers in late spring to early summer.

somewhat sparse heads of lilac flowers. 'Silver Queen', also known as 'Silver Strike', is a white-variegated form, and golden-variegated thyme was the old Elizabethan 'embroidered thyme'. 'Lime' is a low-growing fresh green variety with a tangy lime scent.

Broad-leafed thyme has broadly elliptical leaves with the true thyme fragrance and interrupted inflorescences with whorls of mauve flowers. Varieties include 'Oregano' or 'Pizza' thyme, which is often listed as *T. nummularium*; 'Pennsylvania Tea', with broad leaves and a gentle flavour that's ideal for tisanes; and 'Bertram Anderson' syn. 'Archer's Gold', with pink flowers and bright golden foliage in summer.

Winter-flowering thyme (*T. hyemalis*) forms a small, densely clothed grey bush and is harvested for commercial dried thyme and essential oil.

A number of thymes are popular as much for their long and profuse flowering and dense matting habit as for their fragrance.

Mother of thyme (*T. serpyllum*) has been divided taxonomically into two species, previously classified as subspecies — *T. serpyllum* and *T. quinquecostatus*, with reddish stems. Many popular varieties of carpeting thymes have been developed from the latter, including red-flowered 'Coccineus', 'Minimus' and 'Snowdrift'.

Woolly thyme (*T. pseudolanuginosis*) has soft, grey, dense foliage. Hybrid carpeting varieties also include 'Coconut' and gold-speckled, lemon-scented 'Doone Valley'. 'Porlock' and 'Westmoreland' (Turkey) thyme are both robust culinary varieties.

• **Growing** Thymes require good drainage and a sunny position. There are no pests or diseases of significance if grown in full sun. Substances leached from the leaves of thyme inhibit surrounding plant growth, reducing weed and grass competition.

• **Harvesting and storing** Harvest sprigs at any time for use in cooking. Thyme is low in moisture and easily air-dried out of direct sunlight. It retains its flavour.

In ancient Greece thyme was a symbol of courage and was burned as incense in temples.

🌿 Herbal medicine

Thymus vulgaris. Parts used: leaves, flowering tops. Thyme has potent antimicrobial properties, attributed to the high content of essential oil found in the plant. Thyme also possesses a muscle-relaxant effect and an ability to thin mucus in the lungs, making it easier to expel. These combined effects make thyme a formidable remedy when it comes to the treatment of respiratory conditions, such as colds and flus. Thyme can also be used as a gargle for sore throats and tonsillitis. To use, infuse up to 1 teaspoon (4 g) dried thyme leaves or 2 teaspoons fresh leaves in boiling water. Drink up to 3 cups per day.

In addition, thyme alleviates the symptoms of indigestion, such as gas, bloating and cramps, and its antimicrobial action can also be helpful in treating gastrointestinal infections.

Do not use thyme in greater than culinary quantities and do not use the essential oil if you are pregnant or breastfeeding.

🌿 Around the home

Thyme essential oil is a great addition to cleaning products and disinfectant sprays. For a powerful and fresh-smelling bathroom cleaning spray, mix ¼ teaspoon each of lemon, bergamot, pine, thyme, citronella and tea-tree essential oils with 2 teaspoons vinegar, 1 tablespoon cloudy ammonia and 1 litre water. Then, to this solution add 2 tablespoons bicarbonate of soda and shake until well combined.

Use thyme essential oil in an oil diffuser in a sick room for its antibacterial qualities and soothing aroma.

🌿 Cooking

Various types — including lemon thyme and caraway thyme — have the flavour suggested by their names. Lemon thyme and common thyme, with their warm, pleasant aromas, are the ones commonly used in cooking, but it's well worth trying other varieties.

Thyme is a major culinary herb in Europe, where it shines in slow-cooked casseroles and dishes containing meat, poultry or game. It can be assertive and dominate other milder flavours, so robust companions, such as onions, red wine and garlic work well. Use thyme in terrines, pâtés, meat pies, marinades (especially for olives), eggplant and tomato dishes, and thick vegetable-based soups.

Dried thyme is often used in the jambalayas and gumbos of Creole and Cajun cooking.

Lemon thyme (*Thymus* x *citriodorus*)

Thyme and goat's cheese muffins

2 cups (300 g) plain flour

1 1/2 teaspoons baking powder

1 tablespoon sugar

1/2 teaspoon bicarbonate of soda

1 tablespoon finely chopped fresh thyme

3 tablespoons finely chopped fresh flat-leaf parsley

100 g goat's cheese, crumbled

1 large egg

1 1/4 cups (310 ml) buttermilk

50 g butter, melted

1 Preheat oven to 200°C. Sift flour, baking powder, sugar and bicarbonate of soda into large bowl. Add remaining ingredients; mix until well combined.

2 Spoon mixture into lightly oiled 12–hole standard muffin tin. Bake 15 to 18 minutes, or until muffins are cooked. Turn out onto wire rack to cool.

MAKES 12

Turmeric

Turmeric has a long history of medicinal use. Studies show it may help in reducing the risk of developing certain cancers. Its rhizomes add a golden colour to curries.

· ·

Latin name *Curcuma longa* Zingiberaceae
Part used Rhizomes

The flowers are accompanied by pale green lower bracts and pink to purple upper bracts.

🍃 Gardening

A member of the ginger family, turmeric is native to tropical Southeast Asia. It forms a dense clump of aromatic foliage to about 1 m, spreading by rhizomes that are brown with bright yellow flesh. The flowers are borne in dense spikes with yellow and white to orange tubular flowers. The leaves are simple and the lamina extends to the base of the stems. There are ornamental forms of *C. longa*, including 'Bright White', 'Jamaican Red' and 'Vietnamese Orange'.

Turmeric (*Curcuma longa*)

• **Growing** Turmeric requires a rich, moist soil and consistently warm temperatures in order to flourish. Plants die back underground each winter and will survive some frosts. Propagate from sections of rhizome and divide each year. Turmeric repels ants.
• **Harvesting and storing** Boil the rhizomes for several hours before drying and powdering.

🍃 Herbal medicine

Curcuma longa. Part used: rhizome. Turmeric has a long history of use in Eastern traditional medicinal systems, where it is regarded as an excellent tonic and blood purifier and an effective remedy for inflammatory conditions such as arthritis, skin conditions, including psoriasis, and digestive and liver disorders. Extensive scientific research and clinical trials are providing supportive evidence for its therapeutic effects.

The rhizome contains a compound called curcumin, which is responsible for the vivid yellow colour and has also been shown to be involved in many of turmeric's medicinal effects. Potent anti-oxidant and anti-inflammatory properties have been identified, as well as a protective effect on the liver and an ability to increase bile secretion. Turmeric has also been shown to reduce harmful cholesterol levels in the blood and reduce the development of hardened and blocked arteries. Recent research has also led to the discovery of a remarkable range of potential anti-cancer effects.

Clinical trials have shown turmeric is effective in reducing the symptoms of rheumatoid arthritis and post-operative inflammation. It has also been shown to be effective in the treatment of indigestion, stomach ulcers and inflammatory bowel conditions, such as Crohn's disease and ulcerative colitis.

In addition, studies on large populations have shown that the consumption of large quantities of turmeric is associated with a reduced risk of developing certain cancers and slowing the growth of existing cancers. Researchers have also found that turmeric holds promise in the treatment of Alzheimer's disease.

You can buy commercial preparations of curcumin, turmeric's active compound. For the safe and appropriate medicinal use of turmeric, consult a healthcare professional. Do not use turmeric in doses greater than culinary quantities if you are pregnant or breastfeeding.

🍃 Cooking

Buy plump, firm, clean rhizomes. They should have a warm, mild aroma and an earthy, musky flavour. Turmeric can be used fresh or dried and ground, and adds a brilliant yellow colour to foods. It is used in curry powders and pastes, pickles and chutneys, vegetable, rice and lentil dishes (especially in India, where it often partners potatoes and cauliflower), and with poultry, fish and shellfish. It is also an ingredient in the Moroccan spice blend chermoula (see *page 132*).

Fresh turmeric

Fresh turmeric's flavour is subtle, earthy and slightly bitter, but it's much more flavoursome than dried turmeric. Like the dried version, it gives a wonderful yellow hue to dishes such as curries, stir-fries and vegetable soups. Wear disposable plastic gloves to peel and grate it, as it will stain your hands. To store, wrap fresh unpeeled turmeric in foil or damp paper towel, then put in a ziplock plastic bag and keep in the refrigerator for up to 3 weeks.

Chicken with turmeric, beans and basil

7 chicken tenderloins or 2 large skinless chicken
   breasts (about 500 g in total), cut into thin strips
2 tablespoons vegetable oil
3 teaspoons grated fresh ginger
3 cm piece fresh turmeric, grated,
   or 1 teaspoon dried ground turmeric
1 small red onion, halved, cut into very fine wedges
350 g green beans, trimmed, cut into 4 cm lengths
juice of 1 lime
1 tablespoon fish sauce or salt-reduced soy sauce
½ cup (15 g) small fresh basil leaves
½ cup (80 g) cashew nuts, toasted

1 Mix chicken strips in a bowl with 1 tablespoon oil.

2 Heat a wok or large frying pan over high heat until hot. Stir-fry half the chicken 3 to 4 minutes, until well browned and just cooked through. Transfer to a plate and keep warm. Reheat wok and cook remaining chicken; transfer to plate.

3 Reheat wok and add remaining oil. Stir-fry ginger, turmeric and onion 1 to 2 minutes. Add beans and stir-fry 2 to 3 minutes, or until tender.

4 Return chicken to wok and toss to warm through. Stir in lime juice, fish sauce and most of the basil. Serve garnished with remaining basil and cashews.

SERVES 4

Valerian

In medieval times the calming properties of valerian were so highly regarded that it was known as 'all heal', and was used to treat a wide range of nervous disorders.

....

Latin name *Valeriana officinalis* Valerianaceae
Part used Root

Valerian (*Valeriana officinalis*) bears clusters of white flowers tinged with pink, followed by tiny seeds.

🍃 Gardening

Valerian (*V. officinalis*) is a herbaceous perennial forming a large basal rosette of dark green, fern-like leaves. The tall flowering stem bears large, dense pale pink to pure white heads of sweet-scented flowers. But this is the only sweet-smelling part of the plant, both the leaves and root release an unpleasant odour when crushed. The root yields an essential oil that is used commercially for such purposes as flavouring tobacco and beer. Medicinally, valerian was praised by Arab physicians, was used by Hippocrates in ancient Greece and was a favourite of medieval herbalists.

Chinese medicine has employed several additional species, such as *V. coreana*, *V. fauriei*, *V. amurensis* and *V. stubendorfi*, for indications similar to those used in the West. Note that red valerian or kiss-me-quick is *Centranthus ruber*, which is of no value medicinally.

- **Growing** Native to Western Europe, valerian prefers a cool root run, a sunny to lightly shaded position, and a moist, well-composted, well-drained loam. The plant is propagated by seed sown in spring, scattered over the propagation mix and gently pressed down, as the seed requires light to germinate. Transplant 60 to 70 cm apart. Cats are attracted by valerian leaves and roots, so you may need to provide protection for young plants.
- **Harvesting and storing** Lift the rhizomes in their second year in early spring, then rinse gently and dry them in a cool (100°C) fan-forced oven with the oven door left ajar. Grind if desired.

Valerian (*Valeriana officinalis*)

🌿 Herbal medicine

Valeriana officinalis. Part used: root. Valerian has been used medicinally as a remedy for aiding sleep and relaxation for hundreds of years. Pharmacological studies on the plant have confirmed its sedative effects on the nervous system as well as its relaxant action on muscles. It is rarely associated with side-effects.

A number of clinical trials have assessed the efficacy of valerian on its own or in combination with other relaxing herbs for insomnia, when there is difficulty falling asleep and/or sleep that is easily disturbed. The results of these trials are mixed and may be the result of large variations in the dose and preparation of valerian used as well as how long it was taken for; however, they are strongly suggestive of positive effects on sleep, particularly if taken consistently for more than 2 weeks.

Valerian root has a distinctive odour that cats and rats find irresistible.

A small number of human trials have also shown a beneficial effect of valerian in alleviating the symptoms of anxiety and mental stress.

Valerian's calming effect on nerves and muscles explains the traditional use of the herb for gastro-intestinal cramps, period pains and headaches as well, particularly when they are related to nervousness and tension.

Commercial preparations of valerian are available. For the safe and appropriate use of valerian, consult your healthcare professional. Do not use valerian if you are pregnant or breastfeeding.

The Pied Piper's power

It is not only cats that are entranced by the scent of valerian. Rats, too, find it so enticing that in past times valerian root was used by rat-catchers to bait their traps. Indeed, it is suggested that valerian, and not a magic pipe, was the attractant used by the Pied Piper to rid the medieval German milling town of Hamelin of the plague of rodents that in 1284 threatened to devour its food supplies.

But the townspeople did not keep their promise to pay the piper for his services and in retaliation he used his magic to lure away their children.

A 15th-century manuscript gave the following account of the event:

'In the year of 1284, on the day of Saints John and Paul, on the 26th of June, by a piper, clothed in many kinds of colours, 130 children born in Hamelin were seduced, and lost at the place of execution near the koppen (hill)'.

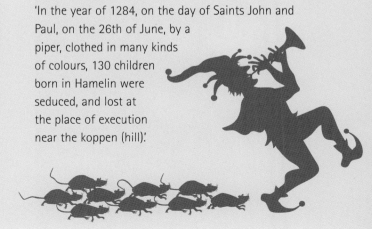

Vervain

Vervain was once considered the most magical of all herbs, and was used in spells and potions for divination, crop fertility, prosperity, love and protection from evil.

....

Latin name *Verbena officinalis* Verbenaceae
Also known as Devils' bane, enchanter's plant, herb of grace, herb of the cross, herb Venus, holy herb, pidgeonweed (it is a bird attractant), simpler's joy, tears of Isis
Parts used Aerial parts

🌿 Gardening

Vervain is native to Europe, Asia and Africa. A slender perennial growing to 1.2 m, it is found on dry, stony ground such as roadsides. The leaves are coarsely and irregularly toothed, and the slender, branched flowering spikes bear small tubular lavender flowers. Blue vervain (*V. hastate*) finds similar uses. Pineapple verbena (*Nashia inaguensis*, family Verbenaceae) is used as a herbal tea.

Devil's bane

Derived from the Celtic *ferfaen*, from *fer*, 'to drive away' and *faen*, 'a stone', vervain has a multitude of religious, cultural and magical associations. For instance, the names herb of the cross, holy herb and devil's bane derive from vervain's reputation for staunching Christ's wounds on the cross, and it was also used in sacrifice and purification ceremonies by the ancient Romans and Druids. In more recent times, the Iroquois people of North America used a concoction of smashed blue vervain (*Verbena hastate*) leaves to make an obnoxious person go away.

• **Growing** Grow plants 30 cm apart, in full sun, in well-drained soil. Sow seed in spring. Germination is erratic and can take 4 weeks.
• **Harvesting and storing** Harvest the green tops just before the flowers open and air-dry them.

🌿 Herbal medicine

Verbena officinalis. Parts used: aerial parts. Vervain has both calming and restorative effects on the nervous system and an uplifting effect on mood. It can help to relieve nervous exhaustion and depression, and act as a supportive remedy during times of tension and stress, and during recovery from feverish illnesses such as flu. The plant's relaxing effects are also of benefit for any muscular tension in the body, reducing intestinal cramps and easing the discomfort of period pains.

For the safe and appropriate use of vervain, consult your healthcare professional. Do not use vervain if you are pregnant or breastfeeding.

Vervain tea was once believed to protect people from vampires.

Vervain (*Verbena officinalis*)

Viburnum

Viburnum are known for their displays of fragrant spring flowers and colourful autumn leaves. The bark of two species have a herbal use as a muscle relaxant.

Viburnum (*Viburnum opulus*)

Latin name *Viburnum opulus, V. prunifolium*
Caprifoliaceae
Also known as Cramp bark, European cranberry bush, guelder rose (*V. opulus*); American sloe, black haw, stagbush (*V. prunifolium*)
Part used Stem bark (*V. opulus*); stem and root bark (*V. prunifolium*)

Gardening

Cramp bark (*Viburnum opulus*) is a deciduous shrub, with vine-shaped leaves that turn red in autumn and large lacy heads of white flowers borne in late spring.

Black haw (*V. prunifolium*) is a spreading deciduous shrub to small tree. It has rounded leaves and flat-topped lacy heads of reddish buds opening to white flowers, followed by lime green berries that ripen black in autumn. Do not eat the berries of either species.

• **Growing** These are deciduous shrubs for cool to mild climates and prefer an open position and well-drained soil. They are easy to grow from seed. Once established, they have modest drought resistance. Prune after flowering, if required.

• **Harvesting and storing** Peel off the outer bark in strips and dry it.

Herbal medicine

Viburnum opulus. Part used: bark. As its name suggests, cramp bark is effective for most types of muscular tension and can help to relax the muscles of the body after strenuous or ongoing physical activity. It is also prescribed for tension and cramping in the digestive system, for easing the symptoms of indigestion and for calming the spasm and discomfort of period pains.

For the safe and appropriate use of cramp bark, consult your healthcare professional. Do not use cramp bark if you are pregnant or breastfeeding.

Poisonous plants

The berries of *Viburnum opulus* are poisonous, and can cause vomiting and diarrhoea. Other species that should not be grown in a garden that young children can access include poisonous foxgloves (*Digitalis* sp.), which produce tall spires of flowers that fit neatly over the fingers, tempting children to play with them, and monkshood (*Aconitum* sp.), which has a similar flowering habit, and contains an extremely toxic compound, aconite, that was once used to poison arrow tips. In Greek mythology, aconite was created from the slavering mouths of Cerberus, a three-headed dog that guarded the gates of Hades.

The shiny red berries of cramp bark (*Viburnum opulus*) are ornamental, but toxic.

Watercress & nasturtium

Watercress is cultivated for its attractiveness as a garnish as well as the bite it gives to soups, pesto, salads, sandwiches and vegetable juices. It is high in vitamin C and folic acid.

....

Latin name *Nasturtium officinale, Tropaeolum majus* Brassicaceae
Parts used Leaves, young stems (watercress); aerial parts (nasturtium)

Watercress (*Nasturtium officinale*)

Gardening

Watercress (*Nasturtium officinale*) is a semi-aquatic perennial herb found wild in streams passing through chalk soils. The cultivated form, now usually grown hydroponically, is preferred, as wild watercress is often a refuge for liver flukes (*Fasciola hepatica*) in areas where sheep graze. The plant has compound green leaves, a hollow stem and insignificant white flowers. It is notably more bitter when flowering.

Nasturtium or Indian cress (*Tropaeolum majus*) has large, shield-shaped, peppery leaves and cheerful, helmet-shaped flowers in yellow, orange and red.

Nasturtium
(*Tropaeolum majus*)

• **Growing** You can grow watercress in pots in a partially shaded position. The large seeds of nasturtium germinate easily in spring, either planted directly into moist soil or germinated in pots and transplanted into a sunny position. To propagate, use tip cuttings grown in regularly changed water, rooted runners or seeds. Grow all other cresses by seed. Water very regularly.
• **Harvesting and storing** Harvest watercress fresh and only use before flowering. Store it at room temperature with its roots in water.

Herbal medicine

Tropaeolum majus. Parts used: aerial parts. Both nasturtium and watercress belong to the same family as horseradish and, like their relative, contain pungent compounds known as mustard oil glycosides, which are responsible for the major medicinal effects of nasturtium.

These compounds possess potent antibacterial and antifungal properties that have particular application in the treatment of infectious conditions of the respiratory and urinary tracts. They can help the body fight off colds, flus and other infections of the lungs as well as cystitis.

The fresh form of the herb appears to have a higher antimicrobial effect than the dried form, and is commonly prepared as an infusion. Applied externally as a poultice or compress, the fresh herb is also used as a local antibacterial agent for cuts and wounds.

Interestingly, fresh nasturtium juice rubbed onto the scalp is said to stimulate hair growth and retard hair loss.

For the safe and appropriate use of nasturtium, consult your healthcare professional. Do not use nasturtium if you are pregnant or breastfeeding.

🍃 Cooking

Rich in anti-oxidants, peppery watercress is one of the most nutritious of salad greens. Its sharp taste also goes well with a citrus dressing. Use watercress in soups, sandwiches and sauces for fish. Cook only briefly to preserve its vitamins.

Nasturtium flowers make an attractive edible garnish and the green leaves add bite to salads. Blend the leaves and flowers with garlic, lemon juice and olive oil to make a peppery pesto.

Other cresses

A number of other species share the hot peppery flavour of watercress and find similar culinary uses. Upland or winter cress (*Barbarea verna*) is a cold-hardy dry-land cress. The cress sold in trays to be clipped for salads is garden cress (*Lepidium sativum*). The cucumber-flavoured Lebanese cress (*Apium nodiflorum*) resembles watercress but is, in fact, a land plant that's related to celery.

Watercress soup

1 tablespoon olive oil
6 spring onions, thinly sliced
700 g washed potatoes, peeled and diced
6 cups (1.5 litres) chicken stock
2 bunches watercress (about 200 g in total), tough stalks removed
2 teaspoons bottled horseradish sauce
½ cup (125 g) crème fraîche or sour cream
2 tablespoons fresh chives, cut into 2 cm lengths

1 Heat oil in large saucepan; sauté spring onions until softened. Add potatoes and stock. Bring to the boil. Reduce heat; simmer 15 to 20 minutes, or until potatoes are tender.

2 Add watercress and horseradish sauce. Add crème fraîche, reserving a little. Stir until watercress wilts. Do not overcook.

3 Using a food processor or hand-held blender, process soup until smooth. Divide among serving bowls, add a swirl of the remaining crème fraîche and sprinkle with chives.

SERVES 6

A garden with a sunny aspect is ideal for a cottage garden featuring herbs.

White horehound

Valued since Egyptian times for its ability to relieve coughs and bronchitis, white horehound is also used in making horehound ale and for flavouring liqueurs.

Latin name *Marrubium vulgare* Lamiaceae
Parts used Leaves, flowering tops

Gardening

White horehound is a perennial with attractive crinkled, downy, grey-white, toothed foliage. The small white flowers, borne in dense clusters in summer, attract bees to the garden. The plant yields an aromatic bitter juice with a distinctive and not unpleasant smell.
- **Growing** White horehound requires a sunny, well-drained position. Sow seed in spring. White horehound has been used as a grasshoppers repellent on various crops.

White horehound (*Marrubium vulgare*)

Passover plate

In late March or in April each year, Jewish people celebrate Passover with a meal that symbolises the flight of the Jews from Egypt. Each item on the plate, or *seder*, represents part of the story of the escape: along with romaine lettuce and grated horseradish, white horehound is one of the bitter herbs eaten to symbolise the harshness of living as a slave in Egypt.

- **Harvesting and storing** Cut down the whole plant just as flowering begins and dry it for herbal use.

Herbal medicine

Marrubium vulgare. Parts used: leaves, flowering tops. Not to be confused with black horehound, which is used for quite different purposes, white horehound is best known for its expectorant properties. It relaxes the bronchial muscles while at the same time encouraging easier removal of mucus from the respiratory tract. To use, infuse up to 1 teaspoon (2 g) of dried flowering tops of white horehound in boiling water; drink 3 cups per day. It has also been used to improve a poor appetite as well as ease symptoms of indigestion.

For the safe and appropriate use of white horehound, consult a healthcare professional. Do not use white horehound if you are pregnant or breastfeeding.

Fresh white horehound can be used to make syrup and candy to ease sore throats and coughs.

Yarrow

Yarrow has been used since ancient times to staunch bleeding and heal wounds. In China, dried yarrow stalks were tossed to consult the *I Ching* (Book of Changes).

Latin name *Achillea millefolium* Asteraceae
Also known as Achillea, bloodwort, carpenter's herb, milfoil
Parts used Leaves, flowers

Gardening

Yarrow is a hardy perennial with feathery leaves and flat-headed, clusters of small white flowers borne on wiry stems to about 70 cm. Its leaves have a refreshing pungent scent that is strangely uplifting to the senses.
- **Growing** Yarrow requires a sunny, well-drained position. It multiplies via underground rhizomes.
- **Harvesting and storing** Harvest the flowering stalks just as they fully open, and dry in small bunches hung upside-down out of direct sunlight. Leaves can be picked at any time.

Yarrow (*Achillea millefolium*)

Herbal antiseptic lotion

Yarrow and comfrey are both superb skin healers. Thyme is antibacterial and antimicrobial while witch hazel is a natural astringent.

2 teaspoons dried thyme
1 teaspoon dried yarrow
1 teaspoon dried comfrey
100 ml boiling water
¼ cup (60 ml) witch hazel

1 Put herbs in a bowl and cover with boiling water. Cover bowl and steep 15 minutes. Strain.

2 Pour liquid into a bottle. Add the witch hazel.

3 To use, shake bottle well and upend onto a cotton-wool ball. Wipe gently over skin. Store in the refrigerator. Use within 10 days.

Herbal medicine

Achillea millefolium. Parts used: aerial parts. Yarrow has long been used on wounds to stop bleeding and reduce inflammation. It is also used to treat feverish conditions such as the early stages of cold or flu where, taken as an infusion (often combined with elderflower), it encourages perspiration and helps to reduce body temperature. Yarrow is also a valuable digestive remedy.

For the safe and appropriate use of yarrow, consult your healthcare professional. Do not use yarrow if you are pregnant or breastfeeding.

Achilles the healer

One of our oldest herbs, yarrow was named for the Greek hero Achilles who, according to Homer's *The Iliad*, used it to staunch the flow of blood from his troops' wounds in the Trojan War. Achilles had been taught how to use plants by Cheiron, a learned centaur. At one point, Eurypylus is wounded and begs Patroclus to 'put the right things on it'. 'Patroclus...crushed a bitter root...and put it on the wound. The root took away all the pain. The blood stopped and the wound dried.'

Herbs reward with colour in the garden and harvests for cooking, household use and medicines.

Index

Page numbers in **bold** print refer to main entries

parsley sauces (recipe), **132**
passionflower, **134–5**
Passionfruit cordial (recipe), 134
Passover, 54, **197**
Pasta with fresh sage, rocket and fetta
    (recipe), 161
pastis, 13
Patroclus, 198
peach sage, 159
pennyroyal, 124, 125, 142
peony, **136**
pepper fennel, 72
peppermint, 124, 125, 126, 160
peppermint essential oil, 125
Peppermint foot scrub, 126
perennial sweet leek *see* elephant garlic
perfumery, **50**, 98, 100, 148, 153, 158,
    166, 167, 171, 173, 180, 182
perilla, **137**
peri peri, 46
Persian cumin *see* caraway
Persillade (recipe), 132
Peruvian black mint, 31
pesto, **19**, 21
pewterwort *see* horsetail
Pied Piper, **191**
pigeonweed *see* vervain
pimentos, 44
pineapple mint, 124
pineapple sage, 159
pineapple verbena, 192
pink savory, 165
pipe tree *see* elder
plantain, **138**
Pliny, 90, 104
poisonous plants, **193**
polyphenols, 180
pomfret cakes, 113
Pontefract cakes, 113
poor man's leek, 79
poppy, **139–41**
Potato and horseradish salad (recipe), 93
potato onions, 78
Potato pizza with chicken and rocket
    (recipe), 147
pot marigold *see* calendula
pot marjoram, 120
pot-pourri, **97**
Potter, Beatrix, 131

poultices, **53**
primrose, **142**
prostate cancer, 75
psoriasis, 10, 28, 30, 75, 145, 174, 188
purple clover *see* red clover
purple echinacea, 62
purple passionflower *see* passionflower
purslane, **144**
Purslane soup (recipe), 144
psyllium, 138

Q

queen of the meadow *see* meadowsweet

R

raki, 13
ras el hanout, 103, 150
rat-tail plantain *see* plantain
rau ram, 54, 124, 125
Raynaud's syndrome, 85
recipes
    Baked fish with ginger and
        spring onions, 83
    Basil oil, 156
    Bavarian cabbage salad, 35
    Beef and potato hotpot, 23
    Berry vinegar, 49
    Caraway crackers, 34
    Chermoula, 132
    Chervil, pea and fetta quiche, 41
    Chicken and vegetable casserole, 179
    Chicken lemongrass skewers, 109
    Chicken with turmeric, beans
        and basil, 189
    Chilli and lime sauce, 47
    Chilli oil, 156
    Chimichurri sauce, 132
    Coriander and chilli butter, 55
    Crushed potatoes flavoured with
        fennel seeds, 73
    Crystallised flowers, 89
    Detox tea, 59
    Elderberry and blackberry jam, 65
    Emerald risotto, 131
    Fennel and saffron vinegar, 49
    Fig cakes, 54
    Harissa, 47
    Herb cocktail, 164
    Herb-crusted leg of lamb, 127

    Herbes de Provence, 165
    herb oils, **156**
    Insalata Caprese, 20
    Lemongrass oil, 156
    Lemon poppy seed cake, 140
    Lovage and fennel omelettes, 117
    Mint jelly, 126
    Nettle soup, 129
    Nuoc cham, 47
    Onion soup, 81
    Palathai, 54
    parsley sauces, **132**
    Passionfruit cordial, 134
    Pasta with fresh sage, rocket and
        fetta, 161
    Persillade, 132
    pesto, 19
    Potato and horseradish salad, 93
    Potato pizza with chicken and
        rocket, 147
    Purslane soup, 144
    Red chilli vinegar, 49
    Rice vinegar with coriander, 49
    Roast leg of lamb with rosemary, 155
    Rosemary oil, 156
    Rose petal jelly, 151
    Savoury dill and caraway scones, 61
    Seafood coconut soup, 77
    Sorrel sauce, 169
    Tabouleh beef wraps, 133
    Tarragon and red wine vinegar, 49
    Thyme and goat's cheese muffins, 187
    Thyme and oregano soufflés, 122
    Vegetarian spring rolls, 56
    Watercress soup, 195
Red chilli vinegar (recipe), 49
red clover, **145**
red madder, 175
red poppy, 139, 140, 141
red valerian, 190
Remembrance Day, **141**
rheumatism, 15, 30, 82, 87, 163
rheumatoid arthritis, 189
Rice vinegar with coriander (recipe), 49
Roast leg of lamb with rosemary (recipe),
    155
rocambole, 78
rocket, **146–7**
Roman chamomile, 38

Herbs: An A–Z Guide to Gardening, Cooking and Health

First published in 2013 by Reader's Digest (Australia) PTY Limited

© 2014 by the Reader's Digest Association, Inc.

ISBN 978-1-4351-5842-9

National Library of Australia Cataloguing-in-Publication data:

Title: Herbs: an A–Z guide to gardening, cooking and health.
ISBN: 978-1-922083-59-3 (paperback)
Notes: Includes index.
Subjects: Herbs. Herb gardening. Herbs–Utilization. Herbs–Therapeutic use. Cooking (Herbs)
Other Authors/Contributors: Reader's Digest (Australia), issuing body
Dewey Number: 635.7

Herbs: An A–Z Guide to Gardening, Cooking and Health contains material first published in *The Complete Book of Herbs* and other Reader's Digest books.

Any images not listed in the photography credits list are the copyright of Reader's Digest

We are committed to both the quality of our products and the service we provide to our customers. We value your comments, so please feel free to contact us.

The Reader's Digest Association, Inc.
Adult Trade Publishing
44 South Broadway
White Plains, NY 10601

For more Reader's Digest products and information, visit our website:

www.rd.com (in the United States)
www.readersdigest.ca (in Canada)

Manufactured in China

3 5 7 9 10 8 6 4 2

WEIGHTS AND MEASURES

Australian weights and measures have been used for this book. 1 cup is the equivalent of 250 ml or 250 g. A tablespoon measure is 20 ml. In New Zealand and South Africa, the cup measure is 235 ml and 235 g and the tablespoon measure is 15 ml. A teaspoon has a 5 ml capacity and is the same for all markets. All cup and spoon measures are level, unless stated otherwise.